THE TRAGEDY OF RICHARD THE THIRD

WITH THE LANDING OF EARL RICHMOND AND THE BATTLE AT BOSWORTH FIELD

EDITED BY

JACK R. CRAWFORD

p.103

NEW HAVEN · YALE UNIVERSITY PRESS
LONDON · HUMPHREY MILFORD
OXFORD UNIVERSITY PRESS · MCMXXVII

THE YALE SHAKESPEARE

EDITED BY

WILBUR L. CROSS   TUCKER BROOKE

PUBLISHED UNDER THE DIRECTION
OF THE
DEPARTMENT OF ENGLISH, YALE UNIVERSITY,
ON THE FUND
GIVEN TO THE YALE UNIVERSITY PRESS IN 1917
BY THE MEMBERS OF THE
KINGSLEY TRUST ASSOCIATION
(SCROLL AND KEY SOCIETY OF YALE COLLEGE)
TO COMMEMORATE THE SEVENTY-FIFTH ANNIVERSARY
OF THE FOUNDING OF THE SOCIETY

CONTENTS

[DRAMATIS PERSONÆ.

KING EDWARD THE FOURTH

EDWARD, *Prince of Wales; afterwards King Edward the Fifth,*
RICHARD, *Duke of York,*
} *Sons to the King*

GEORGE, *Duke of Clarence,*
RICHARD, *Duke of Gloucester, afterwards King Richard the Third,*
} *Brothers to the King*

EDWARD, *a young Son of Clarence*

HENRY, *Earl of Richmond; afterwards King Henry the Seventh*

CARDINAL BOURCHIER, *Archbishop of Canterbury*

THOMAS ROTHERHAM, *Archbishop of York*

JOHN MORTON, *Bishop of Ely*

DUKE OF BUCKINGHAM

DUKE OF NORFOLK

EARL OF SURREY, *his Son*

EARL RIVERS, *Brother to King Edward's Queen*

MARQUESS OF DORSET, *and* LORD GREY, *her Sons*

EARL OF OXFORD

LORD HASTINGS

EARL OF DERBY, *called also* LORD STANLEY

LORD LOVEL

SIR THOMAS VAUGHAN

SIR RICHARD RATCLIFF

SIR WILLIAM CATESBY

SIR JAMES TYRRELL

SIR JAMES BLUNT

SIR WALTER HERBERT

SIR ROBERT BRAKENBURY, *Lieutenant of the Tower*

SIR WILLIAM BRANDON

SIR CHRISTOPHER URSWICK, *a Priest*

Another Priest

Lord Mayor of London

Sheriff of Wiltshire

TRESSEL *and* BERKELEY, *Gentlemen attending on the Lady Anne*

ELIZABETH, *Queen of King Edward the Fourth*

MARGARET, *Widow of King Henry the Sixth*

DUCHESS OF YORK, *Mother to King Edward the Fourth, Clarence, and Richard, Duke of Gloucester*

LADY ANNE, *Widow of Edward, Prince of Wales, Son to King Henry the Sixth; afterwards married to Richard, Duke of Gloucester*

LADY MARGARET PLANTAGENET, *a young Daughter of Clarence*

Lords, and other Attendants; two Gentlemen, a Keeper, a Pursuivant, Scrivener, Citizens, Murderers, Messengers, Ghosts of those murdered by Richard the Third, Soldiers, &c.

SCENE—*England.*]

The Tragedy of Richard the Third,

with the Landing of Earl Richmond, and the Battle at Bosworth Field.

ACT FIRST

Scene One

[London.   A Street]

Enter Richard Duke of Gloucester, solus.

Rich. Now is the winter of our discontent
Made glorious summer by this sun of York;
And all the clouds that lour'd upon our house
In the deep bosom of the ocean buried.   4
Now are our brows bound with victorious wreaths;
Our bruised arms hung up for monuments;
Our stern alarums changed to merry meetings;
Our dreadful marches to delightful measures.   8
Grim-visag'd war hath smooth'd his wrinkled front;
And now,—instead of mounting barbed steeds,
To fright the souls of fearful adversaries,—
He capers nimbly in a lady's chamber   12
To the lascivious pleasing of a lute.
But I, that am not shap'd for sportive tricks,
Nor made to court an amorous looking-glass;
I, that am rudely stamp'd, and want love's majesty   16
To strut before a wanton ambling nymph;

1, 2 winter . . . York; *cf. n.*   6 monuments: *memorial trophies*
7 alarums: *calls to arms*   8 measures: *solemn dances*
9 front: *forehead*
10 barbed: *i.e. having the breasts and flanks armed, properly 'barded'*
11 fearful: *timorous*   12 He capers; *cf. n.*
13 lute: *a stringed instrument*   14 sportive: *amorous*
15 amorous; *cf. n.*   17 ambling: *walking affectedly*

I, that am curtail'd of this fair proportion,
Cheated of feature by dissembling nature,
Deform'd, unfinish'd, sent before my time   20
Into this breathing world, scarce half made up,
And that so lamely and unfashionable
That dogs bark at me, as I halt by them;
Why, I, in this weak piping time of peace,   24
Have no delight to pass away the time,
Unless to see my shadow in the sun
And descant on mine own deformity:
And therefore, since I cannot prove a lover,   28
To entertain these fair well-spoken days,
I am determined to prove a villain,
And hate the idle pleasures of these days.
Plots have I laid, inductions dangerous,   32
By drunken prophecies, libels, and dreams,
To set my brother Clarence and the king
In deadly hate the one against the other:
And if King Edward be as true and just   36
As I am subtle, false, and treacherous,
This day should Clarence closely be mew'd up,
About a prophecy, which says that G
Of Edward's heirs the murtherer shall be.   40
Dive, thoughts, down to my soul: here Clarence comes.

       Enter Clarence and Brakenbury, guarded.

Brother, good day: what means this armed guard
That waits upon your Grace?
       Clar.   His majesty,

18 fair proportion: *goodly form*
19 feature; *cf. n.*   dissembling; *cf. n.*   21 breathing: *living*
22 unfashionable: *unfashionably*
24 weak piping time; *cf. n.*   23 halt: *limp*
29 fair . . . days; *cf. n.*   27 descant: *comment*
31 idle: *trifling*   32 inductions: *initial steps in an undertaking*
33 drunken prophecies; *cf. n.*   36 true and just; *cf. n.*
38 mew'd: *cooped*   39 About: *because of; cf. n.*
43 His majesty; *cf. n.*

Tendering my person's safety, hath appointed   44
This conduct to convey me to the Tower.

   Rich. Upon what cause?

   Clar.   Because my name is George.

   Rich. Alack! my lord, that fault is none of yours;
He should, for that, commit your godfathers.   48
O! belike his majesty hath some intent
That you should be new-christen'd in the Tower.
But what's the matter, Clarence? may I know?

   Clar. Yea, Richard, when I know; but I protest 52
As yet I do not: but, as I can learn,
He hearkens after prophecies and dreams;
And from the cross-row plucks the letter G,
And says a wizard told him that by G   56
His issue disinherited should be;
And, for my name of George begins with G,
It follows in his thoughts that I am he.
These, as I learn, and such like toys as these,   60
Have mov'd his highness to commit me now.

   Rich. Why, this it is, when men are rul'd by women:
'Tis not the king that sends you to the Tower;
My Lady Grey, his wife, Clarence, 'tis she   64
That tempers him to this extremity.
Was it not she and that good man of worship,
Anthony Woodville, her brother there,
That made him send Lord Hastings to the Tower,   68
From whence this present day he is deliver'd?
We are not safe, Clarence; we are not safe.

   Clar. By heaven, I think there is no man secure
But the queen's kindred and night-walking heralds   72
That trudge betwixt the king and Mistress Shore.

44 Tendering: *having regard for*   45 conduct: *escort*
49 belike: *perhaps*   54 hearkens: *inquires*
55 cross-row: *i.e. the alphabet; cf. n.*   58 for: *because*
60 toys: *whims, idle fancies*   62 this: *thus*
65 tempers; *cf. n.*   67 Anthony Woodville; *cf. n.*
72 night-walking heralds; *cf. n.*   73 Mistress Shore; *cf. n.*

Heard you not what a humble suppliant
Lord Hastings was for her delivery?

  Rich. Humbly complaining to her deity   76
Got my lord chamberlain his liberty.
I'll tell you what; I think it is our way,
If we will keep in favour with the king,
To be her men and wear her livery: 80
The jealous o'erworn widow and herself,
Since that our brother dubb'd them gentlewomen,
Are mighty gossips in our monarchy.

  Brak. I beseech your Graces both to pardon me; 84
His majesty hath straitly given in charge
That no man shall have private conference,
Of what degree soever, with your brother.

  Rich. Even so; an 't please your worship, Braken-
    bury,   88
You may partake of anything we say:
We speak no treason, man: we say the king
Is wise and virtuous, and his noble queen
Well struck in years, fair, and not jealous;   92
We say that Shore's wife hath a pretty foot,
A cherry lip, a bonny eye, a passing pleasing tongue;
And that the queen's kindred are made gentlefolks.
How say you, sir? can you deny all this?   96

  Brak. With this, my lord, myself have nought to do.

  Rich. Naught to do with Mistress Shore! I tell
    thee, fellow,
He that doth naught with her, excepting one,
Were best to do it secretly, alone.   100

75 her delivery: *her deliverance of him; cf. n.*   78 way: *course*
81 o'erworn: *faded; cf. n.*
82 dubb'd: *i.e. invested them with the position of*
83 gossips: *meddlesome cronies*   85 straitly: *strictly*
87 degree: *rank*   88 an 't; *cf. n.*
92 Well struck: *advanced; cf. n. on 81 above*
94 bonny: *pleasant, comely*   passing: *exceedingly*
99 naught: *wickedness*

Brak. What one, my lord?

Rich. Her husband, knave. Wouldst thou betray
me?

Brak. I do beseech your Grace to pardon me; and
withal

Forbear your conference with the noble duke.   104

Clar. We know thy charge, Brakenbury, and will
obey.

Rich. We are the queen's abjects, and must obey.

Brother, farewell: I will unto the king;

And whatsoe'er you will employ me in,   108

Were it to call King Edward's widow sister,

I will perform it to enfranchise you.

Meantime, this deep disgrace in brotherhood

Touches me deeper than you can imagine.   112

Clar. I know it pleaseth neither of us well.

Rich. Well, your imprisonment shall not be long;

I will deliver you, or else lie for you:

Meantime, have patience.

Clar.   I must perforce: farewell. 116

Exit Clarence [with Brakenbury, and Guard].

Rich. Go, tread the path that thou shalt ne'er return.

Simple, plain Clarence! I do love thee so

That I will shortly send thy soul to heaven,

If heaven will take the present at our hands.   120

But who comes here? the new-deliver'd Hastings!

Enter Lord Hastings.

Hast. Good time of day unto my gracious lord!

Rich. As much unto my good lord chamberlain!

Well are you welcome to this open air.   124

102 betray: *i.e. trap me into speaking treason*
106 abjects: *i.e. the most servile of her subjects; cf. n.*
109 widow; *cf. n.*   110 enfranchise: *set free*
115 lie for you: *be imprisoned in your stead; cf. n.*

How hath your lordship brook'd imprisonment?

  Hast. With patience, noble lord, as prisoners must:
But I shall live, my lord, to give them thanks
That were the cause of my imprisonment.   128

  Rich. No doubt, no doubt; and so shall Clarence too;
For they that were your enemies are his,
And have prevail'd as much on him as you.

  Hast. More pity that the eagles should be mew'd, 132
While kites and buzzards play at liberty.

  Rich. What news abroad?

  Hast. No news so bad abroad as this at home:
The king is sickly, weak, and melancholy,   136
And his physicians fear him mightily.

  Rich. Now by Saint John, that news is bad indeed.
O! he hath kept an evil diet long,
And over-much consum'd his royal person: 140
'Tis very grievous to be thought upon.
Where is he, in his bed?

  Hast.   He is.

  Rich. Go you before, and I will follow you.

                              Exit Hastings.

He cannot live, I hope; and must not die   144
Till George be pack'd with post-horse up to heaven.
I'll in, to urge his hatred more to Clarence,
With lies well steel'd with weighty arguments;
And, if I fail not in my deep intent,   148
Clarence hath not another day to live:
Which done, God take King Edward to his mercy,
And leave the world for me to bustle in!
For then I'll marry Warwick's youngest daughter. 152
What though I kill'd her husband and her father?

---

133 play; *cf. n.*   137 fear him: *fear for him*
138 Saint John; *cf. n.*   139 diet: *mode of life*
145 post-horse: *i.e. the speediest possible means*
152 Warwick's . . . daughter: *i.e. Lady Anne, the widow of Edward Prince of Wales*

The readiest way to make the wench amends
Is to become her husband and her father:
The which will I; not all so much for love   156
As for another secret close intent,
By marrying her, which I must reach unto.
But yet I run before my horse to market:
Clarence still breathes; Edward still lives and
    reigns: 160
When they are gone, then must I count my gains.
                                        Exit.

Scene Two

[London.   Another Street]

*Enter the corse of Henry the Sixth with Halberds to
    guard it, Lady Anne being the Mourner.*

   Anne. Set down, set down your honourable load,
If honour may be shrouded in a hearse,
Whilst I a while obsequiously lament
Th' untimely fall of virtuous Lancaster.   4
Poor key-cold figure of a holy king!
Pale ashes of the house of Lancaster!
Thou bloodless remnant of that royal blood!
Be it lawful that I invocate thy ghost,   8
To hear the lamentations of poor Anne,
Wife to thy Edward, to thy slaughter'd son,
Stabb'd by the self-same hand that made these
    wounds!
Lo, in these windows that let forth thy life,   12
I pour the helpless balm of my poor eyes.
O, cursed be the hand that made these holes!
Cursed the heart that had the heart to do it!

---

1 Anne; *cf. n.*   3 obsequiously: *mournfully, as befits a funeral*
5 key-cold: *cold in death*   8 invocate: *invoke*
12 windows: *i.e. wounds*   13 helpless: *useless*

Cursed the blood that let this blood from hence!   16
More direful hap betide that hated wretch,
That makes us wretched by the death of thee,
Than I can wish to wolves, to spiders, toads,
Or any creeping venom'd thing that lives!   20
If ever he have child, abortive be it,
Prodigious, and untimely brought to light,
Whose ugly and unnatural aspect
May fright the hopeful mother at the view;   24
And that be heir to his unhappiness!
If ever he have wife, let her be made
More miserable by the death of him
Than I am made by my young lord and thee!   28
Come, now towards Chertsey with your holy load,
Taken from Paul's to be interred there;
And still, as you are weary of this weight,
Rest you, whiles I lament King Henry's corse.   32

    [*The Bearers take up the corpse and advance.*]

     Enter Richard Duke of Gloucester.

  Rich. Stay, you that bear the corse, and set it down.
  Anne. What black magician conjures up this fiend,
To stop devoted charitable deeds?
  Rich. Villains! set down the corse; or, by Saint
    Paul,   36
I'll make a corse of him that disobeys.
  [*First*] *Gent.* My lord, stand back, and let the coffin
    pass.
  Rich. Unmanner'd dog! stand'st thou when I com-
    mand?
Advance thy halberd higher than my breast,   40

17 hap: *fortune*   19 wolves; *cf. n.*
22 Prodigious: *abnormal, monstrous*
25 unhappiness: *disposition to mischief*   29 Chertsey; *cf. n.*
34 black magician: *i.e. one in league with the devil*
35 devoted: *devout*   40 halberd: *a spear with a cutting blade*

Or, by Saint Paul, I'll strike thee to my foot,
And spurn upon thee, beggar, for thy boldness.

               [*The Bearers set down the coffin.*]

   Anne. What! do you tremble? are you all afraid?
Alas! I blame you not; for you are mortal,   44
And mortal eyes cannot endure the devil.
Avaunt, thou dreadful minister of hell!
Thou hadst but power over his mortal body,
His soul thou canst not have: therefore, be gone.   48
   Rich. Sweet saint, for charity, be not so curst.
   Anne. Foul devil, for God's sake hence, and trouble
us not;
For thou hast made the happy earth thy hell,
Fill'd it with cursing cries and deep exclaims.   52
If thou delight to view thy heinous deeds,
Behold this pattern of thy butcheries.
O, gentlemen, see! see! dead Henry's wounds
Open their congeal'd mouths and bleed afresh.   56
Blush, blush, thou lump of foul deformity,
For 'tis thy presence that exhales this blood
From cold and empty veins, where no blood dwells.
Thy deed, inhuman and unnatural,   60
Provokes this deluge most unnatural.
O God! which this blood mad'st, revenge his death;
O earth! which this blood drink'st, revenge his death;
Either heaven with lightning strike the murtherer
    dead,   64
Or earth, gape open wide, and eat him quick,
As thou dost swallow up this good king's blood,
Which his hell-govern'd arm hath butchered!
   Rich. Lady, you know no rules of charity,   68
Which renders good for bad, blessings for curses.

---

49 curst: *malignant, shrewish*   52 exclaims: *exclamations*
54 pattern: *example*   56 Open . . . afresh; *cf. n.*
58 exhales: *draws forth*   65 quick: *alive*

Anne. Villain, thou know'st nor law of God nor man:
No beast so fierce but knows some touch of pity.

Rich. But I know none, and therefore am no beast. 72

Anne. O, wonderful, when devils tell the truth!

Rich. More wonderful when angels are so angry.
Vouchsafe, divine perfection of a woman,
Of these supposed crimes, to give me leave,   76
By circumstance, but to acquit myself.

Anne. Vouchsafe, diffus'd infection of man,
Of these known evils, but to give me leave,
By circumstance, to curse thy cursed self.   80

Rich. Fairer than tongue can name thee, let me have
Some patient leisure to excuse myself.

Anne. Fouler than heart can think thee, thou canst make
No excuse current, but to hang thyself.   84

Rich. By such despair I should accuse myself.

Anne. And by despairing shalt thou stand excus'd
For doing worthy vengeance on thyself,
That didst unworthy slaughter upon others.   88

Rich. Say that I slew them not.

Anne.   Then say they were not slain:
But dead they are, and, devilish slave, by thee.

Rich. I did not kill your husband.

Anne.   Why, then he is alive.

Rich. Nay, he is dead; and slain by Edward's hand. 92

Anne. In thy foul throat thou liest: Queen Margaret saw
Thy murd'rous falchion smoking in his blood;

70 nor . . . nor: *neither . . . nor*   71 touch: *sensation, feeling*
76 crimes; *cf. n.*
77 circumstance: *circumstantial evidence*   but: *only*
78 diffus'd: *disorderly*(?); *cf. n.*   79 Of; *cf. n.*
82 patient: *tranquil*   84 current: *sterling, genuine*
92 Edward's hand; *cf. n.*   94 falchion: *curved sword*

The which thou once didst bend against her breast,
But that thy brothers beat aside the point.   96
  Rich. I was provoked by her sland'rous tongue,
That laid their guilt upon my guiltless shoulders.
  Anne. Thou wast provoked by thy bloody mind,
That never dreamt on aught but butcheries.   100
Didst thou not kill this king?
  Rich. I grant ye.
  Anne. Dost grant me, hedge-hog? Then, God grant
    me too
Thou mayst be damned for that wicked deed!   104
O! he was gentle, mild, and virtuous!
  Rich. The better for the King of heaven that hath
    him.
  Anne. He is in heaven, where thou shalt never come.
  Rich. Let him thank me, that holp to send him
    thither;   108
For he was fitter for that place than earth.
  Anne. And thou unfit for any place but hell.
  Rich. Yes, one place else, if you will hear me name
    it.
  Anne. Some dungeon.
  Rich.   Your bed-chamber.   112
  Anne. Ill rest betide the chamber where thou liest!
  Rich. So will it, madam, till I lie with you.
  Anne. I hope so.
  Rich.   I know so. But, gentle Lady Anne,
To leave this keen encounter of our wits,   116
And fall something into a slower method,
Is not the causer of the timeless deaths
Of these Plantagenets, Henry and Edward,
As blameful as the executioner?   120

95 bend: *direct, aim*
108 holp: *helped*
117 slower: *more deliberate*
                          103 hedge-hog; *cf. n.*
                          113 betide: *befall*
                          118 timeless: *untimely*

Anne. Thou wast the cause, and most accurs'd effect.

Rich. Your beauty was the cause of that effect;
Your beauty, that did haunt me in my sleep
To undertake the death of all the world, 124
So I might live one hour in your sweet bosom.

Anne. If I thought that, I tell thee, homicide,
These nails should rent that beauty from my cheeks.

Rich. These eyes could not endure that beauty's
wrack; 128
You should not blemish it if I stood by:
As all the world is cheered by the sun,
So I by that; it is my day, my life.

Anne. Black night o'ershade thy day, and death thy
life! 132

Rich. Curse not thyself, fair creature; thou art both.

Anne. I would I were, to be reveng'd on thee.

Rich. It is a quarrel most unnatural,
To be reveng'd on him that loveth thee. 136

Anne. It is a quarrel just and reasonable,
To be reveng'd on him that kill'd my husband.

Rich. He that bereft thee, lady, of thy husband,
Did it to help thee to a better husband. 140

Anne. His better doth not breathe upon the earth.

Rich. He lives that loves thee better than he could.

Anne. Name him.

Rich. Plantagenet.

Anne. Why, that was he.

Rich. The self-same name, but one of better nature. 144

Anne. Where is he?

Rich. Here. [*She*] *spits at him.*
Why dost thou spit at me?

Anne. Would it were mortal poison, for thy sake!

121 effect: *agent. In the next line 'effect' has its usual meaning*
127 rent: *rend* 128 wrack: *destruction, ruin*

Rich. Never came poison from so sweet a place.

Anne. Never hung poison on a fouler toad.   148
Out of my sight! thou dost infect mine eyes.

Rich. Thine eyes, sweet lady, have infected mine.

Anne. Would they were basilisks, to strike thee dead!

Rich. I would they were, that I might die at once;   152
For now they kill me with a living death.
Those eyes of thine from mine have drawn salt tears,
Sham'd their aspects with store of childish drops;
These eyes, which never shed remorseful tear;   156
No, when my father York and Edward wept
To hear the piteous moan that Rutland made
When black-fac'd Clifford shook his sword at him;
Nor when thy warlike father like a child   160
Told the sad story of my father's death,
And twenty times made pause to sob and weep,
That all the standers-by had wet their cheeks,
Like trees bedash'd with rain: in that sad time,   164
My manly eyes did scorn an humble tear;
And what these sorrows could not thence exhale,
Thy beauty hath, and made them blind with weeping.
I never su'd to friend, nor enemy;   168
My tongue could never learn sweet smoothing words;
But, now thy beauty is propos'd my fee,
My proud heart sues, and prompts my tongue to speak.
She looks scornfully at him.
Teach not thy lip such scorn, for it was made   172
For kissing, lady, not for such contempt.
If thy revengeful heart cannot forgive,
Lo! here I lend thee this sharp-pointed sword;

148 poison . . . toad; *cf. n.*
155 aspects: *appearance*
163 That: *so that*

151 basilisks; *cf. n.*
158 Rutland; *cf. n.*
169 smoothing: *flattering*

Which if thou please to hide in this true breast,   176
And let the soul forth that adoreth thee,
I lay it naked to the deadly stroke,
And humbly beg the death upon my knee.

     He lays his breast open: she offers at [*it*]
              with his sword.

Nay, do not pause; for I did kill King Henry;   180
But 'twas thy beauty that provoked me.
Nay, now dispatch; 'twas I that stabb'd young Ed-
   ward;   [*She again offers at his breast.*]
But 'twas thy heavenly face that set me on.

           She falls the sword.

Take up the sword again, or take up me.   184
 Anne. Arise, dissembler: though I wish thy death,
I will not be thy executioner.
 Rich. Then bid me kill myself, and I will do it.
 Anne. I have already.
 Rich.   That was in thy rage: 188
Speak it again, and, even with the word,
This hand, which for thy love did kill thy love,
Shall, for thy love, kill a far truer love:
To both their deaths shalt thou be accessary.   192
 Anne. I would I knew thy heart.
 Rich. 'Tis figur'd in my tongue.
 Anne. I fear me both are false.
 Rich. Then never man was true.   196
 Anne. Well, well, put up your sword.
 Rich. Say, then, my peace is made.
 Anne. That shalt thou know hereafter.
 Rich. But shall I live in hope?   200
 Anne. All men, I hope, live so.
 [*Rich.*] Vouchsafe to wear this ring.
 [*Anne.* To take is not to give.]

183 S. d. falls: *lets fall*   194 figur'd: *portrayed*

Rich. Look, how my ring encompasseth thy
    finger,   204
Even so thy breast encloseth my poor heart:
Wear both of them, for both of them are thine.
And if thy poor devoted servant may
But beg one favour at thy gracious hand,   208
Thou dost confirm his happiness for ever.
   Anne. What is it?
   Rich. That it may please you leave these sad designs
To him that hath most cause to be a mourner,   212
And presently repair to Crosby House;
Where, after I have solemnly interr'd
At Chertsey monastery this noble king,
And wet his grave with my repentant tears,   216
I will with all expedient duty see you:
For divers unknown reasons, I beseech you,
Grant me this boon.
   Anne. With all my heart; and much it joys me
    too   220
To see you are become so penitent.
Tressel and Berkeley, go along with me.
   Rich. Bid me farewell.
   Anne.   'Tis more than you deserve;
But since you teach me how to flatter you,   224
Imagine I have said farewell already.
         Exit two [Tressel and Berkeley] with Anne.
  [*Rich.* Sirs, take up the corse.]
   Gent. Towards Chertsey, noble lord?
   Rich. No, to White-Friars; there attend my com-
    ing.   228
                               Exit Corse.

Was ever woman in this humour woo'd?
Was ever woman in this humour won?

213 presently: *immediately*   Crosby House; *cf. n.*
217 expedient: *expeditious*   228 White-Friars; *cf. n.*   229, 230 *Cf. n.*

I'll have her; but I will not keep her long.
What! I, that kill'd her husband, and his father,   232
To take her in her heart's extremest hate;
With curses in her mouth, tears in her eyes,
The bleeding witness of my hatred by;
Having God, her conscience, and these bars against
          me,   236
And I no friends to back my suit withal
But the plain devil and dissembling looks,
And yet to win her, all the world to nothing!
Ha!   240
Hath she forgot already that brave prince,
Edward, her lord, whom I, some three months since,
Stabb'd in my angry mood at Tewkesbury?
A sweeter and a lovelier gentleman,   244
Fram'd in the prodigality of nature,
Young, valiant, wise, and, no doubt, right royal,
The spacious world cannot again afford:
And will she yet abase her eyes on me,   248
That cropp'd the golden prime of this sweet prince,
And made her widow to a woeful bed?
On me, whose all not equals Edward's moiety?
On me, that halts and am misshapen thus?   252
My dukedom to a beggarly denier
I do mistake my person all this while:
Upon my life, she finds, although I cannot,
Myself to be a marvellous proper man.   256
I'll be at charges for a looking-glass,
And entertain a score or two of tailors,
To study fashions to adorn my body:

242 three months; *cf. n.*
245 prodigality of nature: *nature's most prodigal mood*
253 denier: *a small copper coin*   256 proper: *handsome*
257 be . . . for: *buy*   258 entertain: *take into service*

Since I am crept in favour with myself,   260
I will maintain it with some little cost.
But first I'll turn yon fellow in his grave,
And then return lamenting to my love.
Shine out, fair sun, till I have bought a glass,   264
That I may see my shadow as I pass.   *Exit.*

Scene Three

[*London.   A Room in the Palace.*]

Enter the Queen Mother [Elizabeth], Lord Rivers, and Lord Grey.

Riv. Have patience, madam: there's no doubt his
    majesty
Will soon recover his accustom'd health.
  Grey. In that you brook it ill, it makes him worse:
Therefore, for God's sake, entertain good comfort,   4
And cheer his Grace with quick and merry words.
  Q. Eliz. If he were dead, what would betide on me?
  Grey. No other harm but loss of such a lord.
  Q. Eliz. The loss of such a lord includes all harms. 8
  Grey. The heavens have bless'd you with a goodly
    son,
To be your comforter when he is gone.
  Q. Eliz. Ah! he is young; and his minority
Is put unto the trust of Richard Gloucester,   12
A man that loves not me, nor none of you.
  Riv. Is it concluded he shall be protector?
  Q. Eliz. It is determin'd, not concluded yet:
But so it must be if the king miscarry.   16

262 in: *into*   5 quick: *lively*
6 betide on: *become of*   12 *Cf. n.*
15 *Cf. n.*   16 miscarry: *perish*

Enter Buckingham and Derby.

Grey. Here come the Lords of Buckingham and
   Derby.

Buck. Good time of day unto your royal Grace!

Der. God make your majesty joyful as you have
   been!

Q. Eliz. The Countess Richmond, good my Lord of
   Derby,   20

To your good prayer will scarcely say amen.

Yet, Derby, notwithstanding she's your wife,

And loves not me, be you, good lord, assur'd

I hate not you for her proud arrogance.   24

Der. I do beseech you, either not believe

The envious slanders of her false accusers;

Or, if she be accus'd on true report,

Bear with her weakness, which, I think, proceeds   28

From wayward sickness, and no grounded malice.

Q. Eliz. Saw you the king to-day, my Lord of
   Derby?

Der. But now the Duke of Buckingham and I,

Are come from visiting his majesty.   32

Q. Eliz. What likelihood of his amendment, lords?

Buck. Madam, good hope; his Grace speaks cheerfully.

Q. Eliz. God grant him health! did you confer with
   him?

Buck. Ay, madam: he desires to make atonement   36

Between the Duke of Gloucester and your brothers,

And between them and my lord chamberlain;

And sent to warn them to his royal presence.

Q. Eliz. Would all were well! But that will never
   be.   40

I fear our happiness is at the height.

16 S. d. *Cf. n.*   20 Countess Richmond; *cf. n.*
36 atonement: *a reconciliation*   39 warn: *summon*

Enter Richard [with Hastings, and Dorset].

Rich. They do me wrong, and I will not endure it:
Who is it that complains unto the king,
That I, forsooth, am stern and love them not?　　44
By holy Paul, they love his Grace but lightly
That fill his ears with such dissentious rumours.
Because I cannot flatter and look fair,
Smile in men's faces, smooth, deceive, and cog,　　48
Duck with French nods and apish courtesy,
I must be held a rancorous enemy.
Cannot a plain man live and think no harm,
But thus his simple truth must be abus'd　　52
With silken, sly, insinuating Jacks?

Grey. To whom in all this presence speaks your
　　Grace?

Rich. To thee, that hast nor honesty nor grace.
When have I injur'd thee? when done thee wrong?　　56
Or thee? or thee? or any of your faction?
A plague upon you all! His royal grace,—
Whom God preserve better than you would wish!—
Cannot be quiet scarce a breathing-while,　　60
But you must trouble him with lewd complaints.

Q. Eliz. Brother of Gloucester, you mistake the
　　matter.
The king, on his own royal disposition,
And not provok'd by any suitor else,　　64
Aiming, belike, at your interior hatred,
That in your outward action shows itself
Against my children, brothers, and myself,
Makes him to send, that he may learn　　68
The ground [of your ill-will, and so remove it].

48 cog: *cheat*　　　49 Duck: *bow*　　apish: *imitative, false*
53 Jacks: *low-bred fellows*　　　　　　57 faction: *party*
60 breathing-while: *short time*　　61 lewd: *worthless, vile*
63 disposition: *inclination*

Rich. I cannot tell; the world is grown so bad
That wrens make prey where eagles dare not perch:
Since every Jack became a gentleman   72
There's many a gentle person made a Jack.

   Q. Eliz. Come, come, we know your meaning,
    brother Gloucester;
You envy my advancement and my friends'.
God grant we never may have need of you!   76

   Rich. Meantime, God grants that I have need of
    you:
Our brother is imprison'd by your means,
Myself disgrac'd, and the nobility
Held in contempt; while great promotions   80
Are daily given to ennoble those
That scarce, some two days since, were worth a noble.

   Q. Eliz. By him that rais'd me to this careful height
From that contented hap which I enjoy'd,   84
I never did incense his majesty
Against the Duke of Clarence, but have been
An earnest advocate to plead for him.
My lord, you do me shameful injury,   88
Falsely to draw me in these vile suspects.

   Rich. You may deny that you were not the mean
Of my Lord Hastings' late imprisonment.

   Riv. She may, my lord; for—   92

   Rich. She may, Lord Rivers! why, who knows not
    so?
She may do more, sir, than denying that:
She may help you to many fair preferments,
And then deny her aiding hand therein,   96
And lay those honours on your high desert.

71 make prey: *prey*
77 have need of you: *am in trouble because of you*
82 noble: *a coin, with quibble on the usual meaning*
83 careful: *full of cares*
90 mean: *agent*
89 suspects: *suspicions*
95 preferments: *promotions*

What may she not? She may,—ay, marry, may she,—
   Riv. What, marry, may she?
   Rich. What, marry, may she! marry with a king, 100
A bachelor and a handsome stripling too.
I wis your grandam had a worser match.
   Q. Eliz. My Lord of Gloucester, I have too long
    borne
Your blunt upbraidings and your bitter scoffs;   104
By heaven, I will acquaint his majesty
Of those gross taunts that oft I have endur'd.
I had rather be a country servant-maid
Than a great queen, with this condition,   108
To be so baited, scorn'd, and stormed at:
Small joy have I in being England's queen.

Enter old Queen Margaret.

   Q. Mar. [*Aside.*] And lessen'd be that small, God, I
    beseech him!
Thy honour, state, and seat is due to me.   112
   Rich. What! threat you me with telling of the king?
[Tell him, and spare not: look, what I have said]
I will avouch 't in presence of the king:
I dare adventure to be sent to the Tower.   116
'Tis time to speak; my pains are quite forgot.
   Q. Mar. [*Aside.*] Out, devil! I do remember them
    too well:
Thou kill'dst my husband Henry in the Tower,
And Edward, my poor son, at Tewkesbury.   120
   Rich. Ere you were queen, ay, or your husband king,
I was a pack-horse in his great affairs,
A weeder-out of his proud adversaries,
A liberal rewarder of his friends;   124
To royalize his blood I spent mine own.

109 baited: *harassed*   114-116 *Cf. n.*   115 avouch: *maintain*
116 adventure: *venture*   117 pains: *labors*
121 Ere . . . king; *cf. n.*   125 royalize: *make royal*

 Q. Mar. [*Aside.*] Ay, and much better blood than
  his, or thine.

 Rich. In all which time you and your husband Grey
Were factious for the house of Lancaster;   128
And, Rivers, so were you. Was not your husband
In Margaret's battle at Saint Alban's slain?
Let me put in your minds, if you forget,
What you have been ere this, and what you are; 132
Withal, what I have been, and what I am.

 Q. Mar. [*Aside.*] A murtherous villain, and so still
  thou art.

 Rich. Poor Clarence did forsake his father, Warwick,
Ay, and forswore himself,—which Jesu pardon!—136

 Q. Mar. [*Aside.*] Which God revenge!

 Rich. To fight on Edward's party for the crown;
And for his meed, poor lord, he is mew'd up.
I would to God my heart were flint, like Edward's; 140
Or Edward's soft and pitiful, like mine:
I am too childish-foolish for this world.

 Q. Mar. [*Aside.*] Hie thee to hell for shame, and
  leave this world,
Thou cacodemon! there thy kingdom is.   144

 Riv. My Lord of Gloucester, in those busy days
Which here you urge to prove us enemies,
We follow'd then our lord, our sovereign king;
So should we you, if you should be our king. 148

 Rich. If I should be! I had rather be a pedlar.
Far be it from my heart, the thought thereof!

 Q. Eliz. As little joy, my lord, as you suppose
You should enjoy, were you this country's king, 152
As little joy you may suppose in me

128 factious . . . Lancaster; *cf. n.* 130 Margaret's battle; *cf. n.*
136 forswore himself: *repudiated his oath*   139 meed: *reward*
144 cacodemon: *evil spirit*   153 in me: *as regards me*

That I enjoy, being the queen thereof.

  Q. Mar. [*Aside.*] A little joy enjoys the queen
    thereof;

For I am she, and altogether joyless.   156

I can no longer hold me patient.   [*Advancing.*]

Hear me, you wrangling pirates, that fall out

In sharing that which you have pill'd from me!

Which of you trembles not that looks on me?   160

If not that, I being queen, you bow like subjects,

Yet that, by you depos'd, you quake like rebels?

Ah! gentle villain, do not turn away.

  Rich. Foul wrinkled witch, what mak'st thou in my
    sight?   164

  Q. Mar. But repetition of what thou hast marr'd;

That will I make before I let thee go.

  Rich. Wert thou not banished on pain of death?

  Q. Mar. I was; but I do find more pain in banish-
    ment   168

Than death can yield me here by my abode.

A husband and a son thou ow'st to me;

And thou, a kingdom; all of you, allegiance:

This sorrow that I have by right is yours,   172

And all the pleasures you usurp are mine.

  Rich. The curse my noble father laid on thee,

When thou didst crown his warlike brows with paper,

And with thy scorns drew'st rivers from his eyes;   176

And then, to dry them, gav'st the duke a clout

Steep'd in the faultless blood of pretty Rutland.

His curses, then from bitterness of soul

Denounc'd against thee, are all fall'n upon thee;   180

And God, not we, hath plagu'd thy bloody deed.

  Q. Eliz. So just is God, to right the innocent.

---

159 sharing: *dividing*   pill'd: *plundered*   160-162 *Cf. n.*
163 gentle: *precious* (*ironic*)   164 mak'st: *dost*
167 banished; *cf. n.*   174 The curse; *cf. n.*   177 clout: *cloth*

Hast. O! 'twas the foulest deed to slay that babe,
And the most merciless, that e'er was heard of.   184
   Riv. Tyrants themselves wept when it was reported.
   Dors. No man but prophesied revenge for it.
   Buck. Northumberland, then present, wept to see it.
   Q. Mar. What! were you snarling all before I
      came,   188
Ready to catch each other by the throat,
And turn you all your hatred now on me?
Did York's dread curse prevail so much with heaven
That Henry's death, my lovely Edward's death,   192
Their kingdom's loss, my woeful banishment,
Should all but answer for that peevish brat?
Can curses pierce the clouds and enter heaven?
Why then, give way, dull clouds, to my quick
      curses!   196
Though not by war, by surfeit die your king,
As ours by murther, to make him a king!
Edward, thy son, that now is Prince of Wales,
For Edward, our son, that was Prince of Wales,   200
Die in his youth by like untimely violence!
Thyself a queen, for me that was a queen,
Outlive thy glory, like my wretched self!
Long mayst thou live to wail thy children's death, 204
And see another, as I see thee now,
Deck'd in thy rights, as thou art stall'd in mine!
Long die thy happy days before thy death;
And, after many lengthen'd hours of grief,   208
Die neither mother, wife, nor England's queen!
Rivers, and Dorset, you were standers by,—
And so wast thou, Lord Hastings,—when my son
Was stabb'd with bloody daggers: God, I pray him, 212

187 Northumberland; *cf. n.*   194 peevish: *silly*
197 surfeit: *excess of luxurious living*
206 Deck'd: *dressed*   stall'd: *installed*

That none of you may live your natural age,
But, by some unlook'd accident cut off,—
  Rich. Have done thy charm, thou hateful wither'd
    hag!
  Q. Mar. And leave out thee? stay, dog, for thou
    shalt hear me.   216
If heaven have any grievous plague in store,
Exceeding those that I can wish upon thee,
O! let them keep it till thy sins be ripe,
And then hurl down their indignation   220
On thee, the troubler of the poor world's peace.
The worm of conscience still begnaw thy soul!
Thy friends suspect for traitors while thou liv'st
And take deep traitors for thy dearest friends!   224
No sleep close up that deadly eye of thine,
Unless it be while some tormenting dream
Affrights thee with a hell of ugly devils!
Thou elvish-mark'd, abortive, rooting hog!   228
Thou that wast seal'd in thy nativity
The slave of nature and the son of hell!
Thou slander of thy heavy mother's womb!
Thou loathed issue of thy father's loins!   232
Thou rag of honour! thou detested—
  Rich. Margaret!
  Q. Mar.   Richard!
  Rich.   Ha!
  Q. Mar.   I call thee not.
  Rich. I cry thee mercy then, for I did think
That thou hadst call'd me all these bitter names.   236
  Q. Mar. Why, so I did; but look'd for no reply.
O, let me make the period to my curse!
  Rich. 'Tis done by me, and ends in 'Margaret.'

222 begnaw: *gnaw*   228 elvish-mark'd; *cf. n.*   rooting hog; *cf. n.*
229 seal'd: *stamped*
230 slave of nature; *i.e. because branded by nature with a deformity*
238 period: *conclusion*

Q. Eliz. Thus have you breath'd your curse against
  yourself.   240
Q. Mar. Poor painted queen, vain flourish of my
  fortune!
Why strew'st thou sugar on that bottled spider,
Whose deadly web ensnareth thee about?
Fool, fool! thou whet'st a knife to kill thyself.   244
The day will come that thou shalt wish for me
To help thee curse this poisonous bunch-back'd toad.
  Hast. False-boding woman, end thy frantic curse.
Lest to thy harm thou move our patience.   248
  Q. Mar. Foul shame upon you! you have all mov'd
  mine.
  Riv. Were you well serv'd, you would be taught
  your duty.
  Q. Mar. To serve me well, you all should do me
  duty,
Teach me to be your queen, and you my subjects: 252
O, serve me well, and teach yourselves that duty!
  Dor. Dispute not with her, she is lunatic.
  Q. Mar. Peace, Master Marquess! you are malapert:
Your fire-new stamp of honour is scarce current.   256
O that your young nobility could judge
What 'twere to lose it, and be miserable!
They that stand high have many blasts to shake them,
And if they fall, they dash themselves to pieces.   260
  Rich. Good counsel, marry: learn it, learn it, mar-
  quess.
  Dor. It touches you, my lord, as much as me.
  Rich. Ay, and much more; but I was born so high:
Our aery buildeth in the cedar's top,   264

---

241 painted: *feigned, counterfeit*   vain flourish: *empty embellish-*
ment   242 bottled: *i.e. resembling a bottle, swollen*
255 malapert: *impudent*   256 fire-new . . . current; *cf. n.*
264 aery: *brood*

And dallies with the wind, and scorns the sun.

    Q. Mar. And turns the sun to shade; alas! alas!
Witness my son, now in the shade of death;
Whose bright out-shining beams thy cloudy wrath 268
Hath in eternal darkness folded up.
Your aery buildeth in our aery's nest:
O God! that seest it, do not suffer it;
As it was won with blood, lost be it so!   272

    Buck. Peace, peace! for shame, if not for charity.

    Q. Mar. Urge neither charity nor shame to me:
Uncharitably with me have you dealt,
And shamefully my hopes by you are butcher'd.   276
My charity is outrage, life my shame;
And in that shame still live my sorrow's rage!

    Buck. Have done, have done.

    Q. Mar. O princely Buckingham! I'll kiss thy
      hand,   280
In sign of league and amity with thee:
Now fair befall thee and thy noble house!
Thy garments are not spotted with our blood,
Nor thou within the compass of my curse.   284

    Buck. Nor no one here; for curses never pass
The lips of those that breathe them in the air.

    Q. Mar. I will not think but they ascend the sky,
And there awake God's gentle-sleeping peace.   288
O Buckingham! take heed of yonder dog:
Look, when he fawns, he bites; and when he bites,
His venom tooth will rankle to the death.
Have not to do with him, beware of him;   292
Sin, death, and hell have set their marks on him,
And all their ministers attend on him.

    Rich. What doth she say, my Lord of Buckingham?

---

265 dallies: *trifles*   277 My . . . shame; *cf. n.*
284 compass: *range*   285, 286 curses . . . air; *cf. n.*
287 but: *otherwise than that*   291 rankle: *cause a festering wound*

Buck. Nothing that I respect, my gracious lord. 296

Q. Mar. What! dost thou scorn me for my gentle
counsel,
And soothe the devil that I warn thee from?
O! but remember this another day,
When he shall split thy very heart with sorrow,   300
And say poor Margaret was a prophetess.
Live each of you the subject to his hate,
And he to yours, and all of you to God's!   *Exit.*

Buck. My hair doth stand an end to hear her
curses.   304

Riv. And so doth mine. I muse why she's at liberty.

Rich. I cannot blame her: by God's holy mother,
She hath had too much wrong, and I repent
My part thereof that I have done to her.   308

Q. Eliz. I never did her any, to my knowledge.

Rich. Yet you have all the vantage of her wrong.
I was too hot to do somebody good,
That is too cold in thinking of it now.   312
Marry, as for Clarence, he is well repaid;
He is frank'd up to fatting for his pains:
God pardon them that are the cause thereof!

Riv. A virtuous and a Christian-like conclusion, 316
To pray for them that have done scath to us.

Rich. So do I ever, being well-advis'd;
                          Speaks to himself.
For had I curs'd now, I had curs'd myself.

Enter Catesby.

Cates. Madam, his majesty doth call for you;   320
And for your Grace; and yours, my gracious lord.

Q. Eliz. Catesby, I come. Lords, will you go with
me?

298 soothe: *flatter*   304 an: *on*
305 muse: *wonder*   314 frank'd up: *i.e. shut up in a sty*
317 scath: *harm*   321 *Cf. n.*

Riv. We wait upon your Grace.

         Exeunt all but Richard.

 Rich. I do the wrong, and first begin to brawl. 324
The secret mischiefs that I set abroach
I lay unto the grievous charge of others.
Clarence, whom I, indeed, have cast in darkness,
I do beweep to many simple gulls; 328
Namely, to Derby, Hastings, Buckingham;
And tell them 'tis the queen and her allies
That stir the king against the duke my brother.
Now they believe it; and withal whet me 332
To be reveng'd on Rivers, Dorset, Grey;
But then I sigh, and, with a piece of scripture,
Tell them that God bids us do good for evil:
And thus I clothe my naked villainy 336
With odd old ends stol'n forth of holy writ,
And seem a saint when most I play the devil.

    Enter two Murtherers.

But soft! here come my executioners.
How now, my hardy, stout, resolved mates! 340
Are you now going to dispatch this thing?
 Mur. We are, my lord; and come to have the war-
  rant,
That we may be admitted where he is.
 Rich. Well thought upon; I have it here about
  me: [*Gives the warrant.*] 344
When you have done, repair to Crosby-place.
But, sirs, be sudden in the execution,
Withal obdurate; do not hear him plead;
For Clarence is well-spoken, and perhaps 348

324 brawl: *quarrel*   325 set abroach: *set on foot*
328 beweep: *weep over* gulls: *dupes*
329 Namely: *that is to say*   332 whet: *incite*
333 Dorset; *cf. n.*   337 odd old ends: *odds and ends*
339 soft: *stay, stop*   346 sudden: *quick*

May move your hearts to pity, if you mark him.

   Mur. Tut, tut, my lord, we will not stand to prate.
Talkers are no good doers: be assur'd
We go to use our hands and not our tongues.   352

   Rich. Your eyes drop millstones, when fools' eyes
     fall tears:
I like you, lads; about your business straight.
Go, go, dispatch.

   Mur.   We will, my noble lord.

                         [Exeunt.]

Scene Four

[*The Same.   The Tower*]

Enter Clarence and Keeper.

   Keep. Why looks your Grace so heavily to-day?

   Clar. O, I have pass'd a miserable night,
So full of fearful dreams, of ugly sights,
That, as I am a Christian faithful man,   4
I would not spend another such a night,
Though 'twere to buy a world of happy days,
So full of dismal terror was the time.

   Keep. What was your dream, my lord? I pray you,
     tell me.   8

   Clar. Methoughts that I had broken from the
     Tower,
And was embark'd to cross to Burgundy;
And in my company my brother Gloucester,
Who from my cabin tempted me to walk   12
Upon the hatches: there we look'd toward England,
And cited up a thousand heavy times,

---

353 millstones; *cf. n.*   Scene Four S. d. *Cf. n.*
1 heavily: *sorrowfully*   9 Methoughts: *it seemed to me*
10 Burgundy; *cf. n.*
13 hatches: *movable planks forming a kind of deck*
14 cited up: *called to mind*

During the wars of York and Lancaster,
That had befall'n us. As we pac'd along   16
Upon the giddy footing of the hatches,
Methought that Gloucester stumbled; and, in falling,
Struck me, that thought to stay him, overboard,
Into the tumbling billows of the main.   20
O Lord, methought what pain it was to drown:
What dreadful noise of water in mine ears!
What sights of ugly death within mine eyes!
Methoughts I saw a thousand fearful wracks;   24
A thousand men that fishes gnaw'd upon;
Wedges of gold, great anchors, heaps of pearl,
Inestimable stones, unvalu'd jewels,
All scatter'd in the bottom of the sea.   28
Some lay in dead men's skulls; and in those holes
Where eyes did once inhabit, there were crept,
As 'twere in scorn of eyes, reflecting gems,
That woo'd the slimy bottom of the deep,   32
And mock'd the dead bones that lay scatter'd by.
   Keep. Had you such leisure in the time of death
To gaze upon these secrets of the deep?
   Clar. Methought I had; and often did I strive   36
To yield the ghost; but still the envious flood
Stopt in my soul, and would not let it forth
To find the empty, vast, and wandering air;
But smother'd it within my panting bulk,   40
Who almost burst to belch it in the sea.
   Keep. Awak'd you not in this sore agony?
   Clar. No, no, my dream was lengthen'd after life;
O! then began the tempest to my soul.   44
I pass'd, methought, the melancholy flood,

20 main: *sea*   24 wracks: *wrecks*   26 Wedges: *masses*
27 unvalu'd: *priceless*   31 reflecting: *shining*
37 yield the ghost: *i.e. die*   envious: *malicious*
38 Stopt in: *kept in*   40 bulk: *body*
45 melancholy flood; *cf. n.*

With that sour ferryman which poets write of,
Unto the kingdom of perpetual night.
The first that there did greet my stranger soul   48
Was my great father-in-law, renowned Warwick;
Who spake aloud, 'What scourge for perjury
Can this dark monarchy afford false Clarence?'
And so he vanish'd: then came wand'ring by   52
A shadow like an angel, with bright hair
Dabbled in blood; and he shriek'd out aloud,
'Clarence is come,—false, fleeting, perjur'd Clarence,
That stabb'd me in the field by Tewkesbury;—   56
Seize on him, Furies; take him unto torment!'
With that, methought, a legion of foul fiends
Environ'd me, and howled in mine ears
Such hideous cries, that with the very noise   60
I trembling wak'd, and for a season after
Could not believe but that I was in hell,
Such terrible impression made my dream.

   Keep. No marvel, lord, though it affrighted you; 64
I am afraid, methinks, to hear you tell it.

   Clar. Ah Keeper, Keeper! I have done these things,
That now give evidence against my soul,
For Edward's sake; and see how he requites me.   68
O God! if my deep prayers cannot appease thee,
But thou wilt be aveng'd on my misdeeds,
Yet execute thy wrath on me alone:
O, spare my guiltless wife and my poor children!   72
Keeper, I prithee sit by me a while;
My soul is heavy, and I fain would sleep.

   Keep. I will, my lord. God give your Grace good
     rest!   [*Clarence sleeps.*]

46 ferryman: *Charon*   49 father-in-law; *cf. n.*
50 scourge for perjury; *cf. n.*   53 A shadow; *cf. n.*
55 fleeting: *vacillating*   56 stabb'd . . . Tewkesbury; *cf. n.*
64 No . . . though: *it is not strange that*   74 fain: *gladly*

Enter Brakenbury, the Lieutenant.

Brak. Sorrow breaks seasons and reposing hours, 76
Makes the night morning, and the noon-tide night.
Princes have but their titles for their glories,
An outward honour for an inward toil;
And, for unfelt imaginations,   80
They often feel a world of restless cares:
So that, between their titles and low name,
There's nothing differs but the outward fame.

Enter [the] two Murtherers.

1. Mur. Ho! who's here?   84
Brak. What wouldst thou, fellow? and how cam'st
thou hither?
2. Mur. I would speak with Clarence, and
I came hither on my legs.
Brak. What! so brief?   88
1. Mur. 'Tis better, sir, than to be tedious.—
Let him see our commission, and talk no more.

[Brakenbury] Reads.

Brak. I am, in this, commanded to deliver
The noble Duke of Clarence to your hands: 92
I will not reason what is meant hereby,
Because I will be guiltless from the meaning.
There lies the duke asleep, and there the keys.
I'll to the king, and signify to him   96
That thus I have resign'd to you my charge.
1. Mur. You may, sir; 'tis a point of wisdom: fare you well.   *Exit [Brakenbury].*
2. Mur. What! shall we stab him as he 100
sleeps?
1. Mur. No; he'll say 'twas done cowardly,
when he wakes.

---

80 unfelt imaginations: *i.e. what they imagine they might do but are
unable to realize*

2. Mur. Why, he shall never wake until the 104
great judgment day.

1. Mur. Why, then he'll say we stabbed
him sleeping.

2. Mur. The urging of that word 'judg- 108
ment' hath bred a kind of remorse in
me.

1. Mur. What! art thou afraid?

2. Mur. Not to kill him, having a warrant, but 112
to be damn'd for killing him, from the which no
warrant can defend me.

1. Mur. I thought thou hadst been reso-
lute. 116

2. Mur. So I am, to let him live.

1. Mur. I'll back to the Duke of Gloucester,
and tell him so.

2. Mur. Nay, I prithee, stay a little: I hope 120
this passionate humour of mine will change; it
was wont to hold me but while one tells twenty.

1. Mur. How dost thou feel thyself
now? 124

2. Mur. Some certain dregs of conscience are
yet within me.

1. Mur. Remember our reward when the deed's
done. 128

2. Mur. Come, he dies: I had forgot the reward.

1. Mur. Where's thy conscience now?

2. Mur. O, in the Duke of Gloucester's purse. 132

1. Mur. When he opens his purse to give us
our reward, thy conscience flies out.

2. Mur. 'Tis no matter; let it go: there's few
or none will entertain it. 136

109 remorse: *scruple*   121 humour: *mood*   122 tells: *counts*

1. *Mur.* What if it come to thee again?

2. *Mur.* I'll not meddle with it; it makes
a man a coward; a man cannot steal, but it
accuseth him; a man cannot swear, but it checks 140
him; a man cannot lie with his neighbour's wife,
but it detects him: 'tis a blushing shamefac'd
spirit, that mutinies in a man's bosom; it fills
a man full of obstacles; it made me once restore 144
a purse of gold that, by chance, I found; it beggars any man that keeps it; it is turned out of
towns and cities for a dangerous thing; and every
man that means to live well endeavours to 148
trust to himself and live without it.

1. *Mur.* 'Tis even now at my elbow, persuading
me not to kill the duke.

2. *Mur.* Take the devil in thy mind, and 152
believe him not: he would insinuate with thee
but to make thee sigh.

1. *Mur.* I am strong-framed; he cannot pre-
vail with me.   156

2. *Mur.* Spoke like a tall man that respects thy reputation. Come, shall we fall to
work?

1. *Mur.* Take him on the costard with 160
the hilts of thy sword, and then throw him into
the malmsey-butt in the next room.

2. *Mur.* O, excellent device! and make a sop
of him.   164

1. *Mur.* Soft! he wakes.

2. *Mur.* Strike!

1. *Mur.* No, we'll reason with him.

142 shamefac'd: *bashful*
153 him: *refers to conscience*   insinuate: *ingratiate*
157 tall: *doughty, valiant*   160 costard: *head; cf. n.*
161 hilts: *hilt*   162 malmsey: *a kind of wine*   163 sop; *cf. n.*

Clar. Where art thou, keeper? give me a cup 168
of wine.

2. Mur. You shall have wine enough, my lord,
anon.

Clar. In God's name, what art thou? 172

1. Mur. A man, as you are.

Clar. But not, as I am, royal.

1. Mur. Nor you, as we are, loyal.

Clar. Thy voice is thunder, but thy looks are
humble. 176

1. Mur. My voice is now the king's, my looks mine
own.

Clar. How darkly, and how deadly dost thou speak!
Your eyes do menace me: why look you pale?
Who sent you hither? Wherefore do you come? 180

2. Mur. To, to, to—

Clar. To murther me?

Both [*Mur.*] Ay, ay.

Clar. You scarcely have the hearts to tell me so, 184
And therefore cannot have the hearts to do it.
Wherein, my friends, have I offended you?

1. Mur. Offended us you have not, but the king.

Clar. I shall be reconcil'd to him again. 188

2. Mur. Never, my lord; therefore prepare to die.

Clar. Are you drawn forth among a world of men
To slay the innocent? What is my offence?
Where is the evidence that doth accuse me? 192
What lawful quest have given their verdict up
Unto the frowning judge? or who pronounc'd
The bitter sentence of poor Clarence' death?
Before I be convict by course of law, 196
To threaten me with death is most unlawful.

---

178 darkly: *frowningly*   193 quest: *inquest, jury*
196 convict: *convicted*

I charge you, as you hope for any goodness
[By Christ's dear blood shed for our grievous sins,]
That you depart and lay no hands on me: 200
The deed you undertake is damnable.

   1. Mur. What we will do, we do upon command.

   2. Mur. And he that hath commanded is our king.

   Clar. Erroneous vassals! the great King of kings 204
Hath in the table of his law commanded
That thou shalt do no murther: will you, then,
Spurn at his edict and fulfil a man's?
Take heed; for he holds vengeance in his hand,   208
To hurl upon their heads that break his law.

   2. Mur. And that same vengeance doth he hurl on
     thee,
For false forswearing and for murther too:
Thou didst receive the sacrament to fight   212
In quarrel of the house of Lancaster.

   1. Mur. And, like a traitor to the name of God,
Didst break that vow, and, with thy treacherous blade
Unripp'dst the bowels of thy sovereign's son.   216

   2. Mur. Whom thou wast sworn to cherish and
     defend.

   1. Mur. How canst thou urge God's dreadful law
     to us,
When thou hast broke it in such dear degree?

   Clar. Alas! for whose sake did I that ill deed?   220
For Edward, for my brother, for his sake:
He sends you not to murther me for this;
For in that sin he is as deep as I.
If God will be avenged for the deed,   224
O! know you yet, he doth it publicly:
Take not the quarrel from his powerful arm;

199 *Cf. n.*   204 Erroneous: *misguided*
207 Spurn at: *oppose contemptuously*
219 dear: *grievous, dire*

He needs no indirect or lawless course
To cut off those that have offended him.   228

  1. Mur. Who made thee then a bloody minister,
When gallant-springing, brave Plantagenet,
That princely novice, was struck dead by thee?

  Clar. My brother's love, the devil, and my rage.   232

  1. Mur. Thy brother's love, our duty, and thy faults,
Provoke us hither now to slaughter thee.

  Clar. If you do love my brother, hate not me;
I am his brother, and I love him well.   236
If you are hir'd for meed, go back again,
And I will send you to my brother Gloucester,
Who shall reward you better for my life
Than Edward will for tidings of my death.   240

  2. Mur. You are deceiv'd, your brother Gloucester
    hates you.

  Clar. O, no! he loves me, and he holds me dear:
Go you to him from me.

  1. Mur.   Ay, so we will.

  Clar. Tell him, when that our princely father
    York   244
Bless'd his three sons with his victorious arm,
[And charg'd us from his soul to love each other,]
He little thought of this divided friendship:
Bid Gloucester think on this, and he will weep.   248

  1. Mur. Ay, millstones; as he lesson'd us to weep.

  Clar. O! do not slander him, for he is kind.

  1. Mur. Right;
As snow in harvest. Come, you deceive yourself.   252
'Tis he that sends us to destroy you here.

  Clar. It cannot be; for he bewept my fortune,
And hugg'd me in his arms, and swore, with sobs,

---

230 gallant-springing; *cf. n.*   231 novice: *youth*
232 My brother's love: *my love of my brother*   234 Provoke: *urge*
249 lesson'd: *taught*   252 snow in harvest; *cf. n.*

That he would labour my delivery.   256
  1. Mur. Why, so he doth, when he delivers you
From this earth's thraldom to the joys of heaven.
  2. Mur. Make peace with God, for you must die, my
      lord.
  Clar. Have you that holy feeling in your souls,   260
To counsel me to make my peace with God,
And are you yet to your own souls so blind,
That you will war with God by murd'ring me?
O, sirs, consider! they that set you on   264
To do this deed, will hate you for the deed.
  2. Mur. What shall we do?
  Clar.   Relent and save your souls.
  1. Mur. Relent? 'Tis cowardly and womanish.
  Clar. Not to relent, is beastly, savage, devilish.   268
Which of you, if you were a prince's son,
Being pent from liberty, as I am now,
If two such murtherers as yourselves came to you,
Would not entreat for life?   272
My friend, I spy some pity in thy looks;
O! if thine eye be not a flatterer,
Come thou on my side, and entreat for me,
As you would beg, were you in my distress.   276
A begging prince what beggar pities not?
  2. Mur. Look behind you, my lord.
  1. Mur. Take that! and that!   *Stabs him.*
                        If all this will not do,
I'll drown you in the malmsey-butt within.   280
                        Exit [*with the body*].
  2. Mur. A bloody deed, and desperately dispatch'd!
How fain, like Pilate, would I wash my hands
Of this most grievous murther.

256 labour: *busy himself to procure*   258 thraldom: *slavery*
270 pent from: *shut up from*   280 malmsey-butt; *cf. n.*
282 Pilate; *cf. n.*

Enter 1. Murtherer.

1. Mur. How now! what mean'st thou, that thou
   help'st me not?   284
By heaven, the duke shall know how slack you have
   been.
2. Mur. I would he knew that I had sav'd his
   brother!
Take thou the fee, and tell him what I say;
For I repent me that the duke is slain.   *Exit.* 288
1. Mur. So do not I: go, coward as thou art.
Well, I'll go hide the body in some hole,
Till that the duke give order for his burial:
And when I have my meed, I will away;   292
For this will out, and then I must not stay.   *Exit.*

ACT SECOND

Scene One

[London.   A room in the Palace]

*Flourish.   Enter the King [Edward IV] sick, the
Queen [Elizabeth], Lord Marquess Dorset, Rivers,
Hastings, Catesby, Buckingham, [Grey,] Wood-
ville [and Others].*

K. Edw. Why, so: now have I done a good day's
   work.
You peers, continue this united league:
I every day expect an embassage
From my Redeemer to redeem me hence;   4
And more at peace my soul shall part to heaven,
Since I have made my friends at peace on earth.

2 united league; *cf. n.*

Rivers and Hastings, take each other's hand;
Dissemble not your hatred, swear your love.   8
   Riv. By heaven, my soul is purg'd from grudging
     hate;
And with my hand I seal my true heart's love.
   Hast. So thrive I, as I truly swear the like!
   K. Edw. Take heed, you dally not before your
     king;   12
Lest he that is the supreme King of kings
Confound your hidden falsehood, and award
Either of you to be the other's end.
   Hast. So prosper I, as I swear perfect love!   16
   Riv. And I, as I love Hastings with my heart!
   K. Edw. Madam, your self is not exempt from this;
Nor you, son Dorset; Buckingham, nor you:
You have been factious one against the other.   20
Wife, love Lord Hastings, let him kiss your hand;
And what you do, do it unfeignedly.
   Q. Eliz. There, Hastings; I will never more remem-
     ber
Our former hatred, so thrive I and mine!   24
   K. Edw. Dorset, embrace him; Hastings, love lord
     marquess.
   Dor. This interchange of love, I here protest,
Upon my part shall be inviolable.
   Hast. And so swear I.   *[They embrace.]* 28
   K. Edw. Now, princely Buckingham, seal thou this
     league
With thy embracements to my wife's allies,
And make me happy in your unity.
   Buck. [*To the Queen.*] Whenever Buckingham doth
     turn his hate   32

7 Rivers and Hastings; *cf. n.*   8 Dissemble: *disguise*
11 So . . . like; *cf. n.*   12 dally: *play a part*
15 Either . . . end; *cf. n.*   20 factious: *quarrelsome*

Upon your Grace, but with all duteous love
Doth cherish you and yours, God punish me
With hate in those where I expect most love!
When I have most need to employ a friend,   36
And most assured that he is a friend,
Deep, hollow, treacherous, and full of guile,
Be he unto me! This do I beg of heaven,
When I am cold in love to you or yours.   40

> *[They] embrace.*

    K. Edw. A pleasing cordial, princely Buckingham,
Is this thy vow unto my sickly heart.
There wanteth now our brother Gloucester here
To make the blessed period of this peace.   44

    Buck. And, in good time, here comes Sir Richard
      Ratcliff and the duke.

Enter Ratcliff and Gloucester.

    Rich. Good morrow to my sovereign king and queen;
And princely peers, a happy time of day!

    K. Edw. Happy, indeed, as we have spent the
      day.   48
Gloucester, we have done deeds of charity;
Made peace of enmity, fair love of hate,
Between these swelling wrong-incensed peers.

    Rich. A blessed labour, my most sovereign lord.   52
Among this princely heap, if any here,
By false intelligence, or wrong surmise,
Hold me a foe;
If I unwillingly, or in my rage,   56
Have aught committed that is hardly borne
To any in this presence, I desire

---

37 most: *am most*   43 wanteth: *is needed*
45 in good time: *at a fortunate moment*   50 of: *instead of*
51 swelling: *inflated with anger*   53 heap: *assembly*
56 unwillingly: *unintentionally*   rage: *unthinking passion*
57 hardly borne: *taken amiss*

To reconcile me to his friendly peace:
'Tis death to me to be at enmity;   60
I hate it, and desire all good men's love.
First, madam, I entreat true peace of you,
Which I will purchase with my duteous service;
Of you, my noble cousin Buckingham,   64
If ever any grudge were lodg'd between us;
Of you, and you, Lord Rivers, and of Dorset,
That all without desert have frown'd on me;
Of you, Lord Woodville, and Lord Scales, of you,   68
Dukes, earls, lords, gentlemen; indeed, of all.
I do not know that Englishman alive
With whom my soul is any jot at odds
More than the infant that is born to-night: 72
I thank my God for my humility.

 Q. Eliz. A holy day shall this be kept hereafter:
I would to God all strifes were well compounded.
My sovereign lord, I do beseech your highness   76
To take our brother Clarence to your grace.

 Rich. Why, madam, have I offer'd love for this,
To be so flouted in this royal presence?
Who knows not that the gentle duke is dead?   80
         They all start.
You do him injury to scorn his corse.

 K. Edw. Who knows not he is dead! who knows he
 is?

 Q. Eliz. All-seeing heaven, what a world is this!

 Buck. Look I so pale, Lord Dorset, as the rest?   84

 Dor. Ay, my good lord; and no man in the presence
But his red colour hath forsook his cheeks.

 K. Edw. Is Clarence dead? the order was revers'd.

 Rich. But he, poor man, by your first order died, 88

---

59 me: *myself*   66 Of . . . Dorset; *cf. n.*
67 without desert: *i.e. without desert on my part*
68 Lord . . . Scales; *cf. n.*   69-72 *Cf. n.*
75 compounded: *settled*   85 presence: *king's company*

And that a winged Mercury did bear;
Some tardy cripple bare the countermand,
That came too lag to see him buried.
God grant that some, less noble and less loyal,   92
Nearer in bloody thoughts, and not in blood,
Deserve not worse than wretched Clarence did,
And yet go current from suspicion.

Enter Earl of Derby.

   Der. A boon, my sovereign, for my service done! 96
   K. Edw. I prithee, peace: my soul is full of sorrow.
   Der. I will not rise, unless your highness hear me.
   K. Edw. Then say at once, what is it thou re-
     quest'st.
   Der. The forfeit, sovereign, of my servant's life; 100
Who slew to-day a riotous gentleman
Lately attendant on the Duke of Norfolk.
   K. Edw. Have I a tongue to doom my brother's
     death,
And shall that tongue give pardon to a slave?   104
My brother kill'd no man, his fault was thought;
And yet his punishment was bitter death.
Who su'd to me for him? who, in my wrath,
Kneel'd at my feet, and bid me be advis'd?   108
Who spoke of brotherhood? who spoke of love?
Who told me how the poor soul did forsake
The mighty Warwick, and did fight for me?
Who told me, in the field at Tewkesbury,   112
When Oxford had me down, he rescu'd me,
And said, 'Dear brother, live, and be a king'?
Who told me, when we both lay in the field,
Frozen almost to death, how he did lap me   116

90 bare: *bore*   91 lag: *late*
93 blood: *relationship*   95 go . . . suspicion; *cf.n.*
104 pardon . . . slave; *cf.n.*   108 be advis'd: *deliberate*
113 Oxford; *cf. n.*   116 lap: *enwrap*

Even in his garments; and did give himself,
All thin and naked, to the numb cold night?
All this from my remembrance brutish wrath
Sinfully pluck'd, and not a man of you   120
Had so much grace to put it in my mind.
But when your carters or your waiting-vassals
Have done a drunken slaughter, and defac'd
The precious image of our dear Redeemer,   124
You straight are on your knees for pardon, pardon;
And I, unjustly too, must grant it you;
But for my brother not a man would speak,
Nor I, ungracious, speak unto myself   128
For him, poor soul. The proudest of you all
Have been beholding to him in his life,
Yet none of you would once beg for his life.
O God! I fear, thy justice will take hold   132
On me and you and mine and yours for this.
Come, Hastings, help me to my closet. Ah, poor
    Clarence!
            Exeunt some with King and Queen [*Hastings,*
                    Rivers, Dorset, and Grey].
    Rich. This is the fruits of rashness. Mark'd you not
How that the guilty kindred of the queen   136
Look'd pale when they did hear of Clarence' death?
O! they did urge it still unto the king:
God will revenge it. Come, lords; will you go
To comfort Edward with our company?   140
    Buck. We wait upon your Grace.   *Exeunt.*

130 beholding: *under obligation*

Scene Two

[The Same.   A Room in the Palace]

Enter the old Duchess of York, with the two children
of Clarence [Edward and a daughter].

Edw. Good grandam, tell us, is our father dead?
Duch. No, boy.
Daugh. Why do you weep so oft, and beat your
    breast,
And cry—'O Clarence, my unhappy son'?   4
Edw. Why do you look on us, and shake your head,
And call us orphans, wretches, castaways,
If that our noble father were alive?
Duch. My pretty cousins, you mistake me both;   8
I do lament the sickness of the king,
As loath to lose him, not your father's death;
It were lost sorrow to wail one that's lost.
Edw. Then you conclude, my grandam, he is dead. 12
The king, mine uncle, is to blame for it:
God will revenge it; whom I will importune
With earnest prayers all to that effect.
Daugh. And so will I.   16
Duch. Peace, children, peace! the king doth love
    you well.
Incapable and shallow innocents,
You cannot guess who caus'd your father's death.
Edw. Grandam, we can; for my good uncle Glouces-
    ter   20
Told me, the king, provok'd to 't by the queen,
Devis'd impeachments to imprison him:
And when my uncle told me so, he wept,

6 castaways; *cf. n.*   8 cousins: *relatives, here grandchildren*
18 Incapable: *without power of understanding*
22 impeachments: *accusations*

And pitied me, and kindly kiss'd my cheek;   24
Bade me rely on him, as on my father,
And he would love me dearly as a child.
   Duch. Ah! that deceit should steal such gentle
     shape,
And with a virtuous visor hide deep vice.   28
He is my son, ay, and therein my shame,
Yet from my dugs he drew not this deceit.
   Edw. Think you my uncle did dissemble, grandam?
   Duch. Ay, boy.   32
   Edw. I cannot think it. Hark! what noise is this?

*Enter the Queen [Elizabeth] with her hair about
    her ears; Rivers and Dorset after her.*

   Q. Eliz. Ah! who shall hinder me to wail and weep,
To chide my fortune, and torment myself?
I'll join with black despair against my soul,   36
And to myself become an enemy.
   Duch. What means this scene of rude impatience?
   Q. Eliz. To make an act of tragic violence:
Edward, my lord, thy son, our king, is dead!   40
Why grow the branches when the root is gone?
Why wither not the leaves that want their sap?
If you will live, lament: if die, be brief,
That our swift-winged souls may catch the king's;   44
Or, like obedient subjects, follow him
To his new kingdom of ne'er-changing night.
   Duch. Ah! so much interest have I in thy sorrow
As I had title in thy noble husband.   48
I have bewept a worthy husband's death,
And liv'd with looking on his images;
But now two mirrors of his princely semblance
Are crack'd in pieces by malignant death,   52

24 *Cf. n.*   27 shape: *outward appearance*   28 visor: *mask*
40 Edward; *cf. n.*   50 images: *i.e. children*

And I for comfort have but one false glass,
That grieves me when I see my shame in him.
Thou art a widow; yet thou art a mother,
And hast the comfort of thy children left [thee]: 56
But death hath snatch'd my husband from mine arms,
And pluck'd two crutches from my feeble hands,
Clarence and Edward. O! what cause have I—
Thine being but a moiety of my moan— 60
To overgo thy woes, and drown thy cries!

    Edw. Ah, aunt, you wept not for our father's death;
How can we aid you with our kindred tears?

    Daugh. Our fatherless distress was left un-
      moan'd; 64
Your widow-dolour likewise be unwept.

    Q. Eliz. Give me no help in lamentation;
I am not barren to bring forth complaints:
All springs reduce their currents to mine eyes, 68
That I, being govern'd by the watery moon,
May send forth plenteous tears to drown the world!
Ah, for my husband! for my dear Lord Edward!

    Chil. Ah, for our father! for our dear Lord
      Clarence! 72

    Duch. Alas, for both! both mine, Edward and
      Clarence!

    Q. Eliz. What stay had I but Edward? and he's
      gone.

    Chil. What stay had we but Clarence? and he's
      gone.

    Duch. What stays had I but they? and they are
      gone. 76

    Q. Eliz. Was never widow had so dear a loss.

    Chil. Were never orphans had so dear a loss.

---

53 false glass: *i.e. Richard*   60 moiety: *fractional part, half*
61 overgo: *exceed*   63 kindred tears: *i.e. tears of kinsmen*
65 widow-dolour: *widow's grief*   67 to: *in capacity to*
68 reduce: *bring back*   70 *Cf. n.*   74 stay: *support*

Duch. Was never mother had so dear a loss.
Alas! I am the mother of these griefs: 80
Their woes are parcell'd, mine is general.
She for an Edward weeps, and so do I;
I for a Clarence weep, so doth not she:
These babes for Clarence weep, [and so do I;   84
I for an Edward weep,] so do not they:
Alas! you three, on me, threefold distress'd,
Pour all your tears; I am your sorrow's nurse,
And I will pamper it with lamentation.   88
    Dor. Comfort, dear mother: God is much displeas'd
That you take with unthankfulness his doing.
In common worldly things 'tis call'd ungrateful,
With dull unwillingness to repay a debt   92
Which with a bounteous hand was kindly lent;
Much more to be thus opposite with heaven,
For it requires the royal debt it lent you.
    Riv. Madam, bethink you, like a careful mother, 96
Of the young prince your son: send straight for him;
Let him be crown'd; in him your comfort lives.
Drown desperate sorrow in dead Edward's grave,
And plant your joys in living Edward's throne.   100

*Enter Richard [Duke of Gloucester], Buckingham,
    Derby, Hastings, and Ratcliff.*

    Rich. Sister, have comfort: all of us have cause ✓
To wail the dimming of our shining star;
But none can help our harms by wailing them.
Madam, my mother, I do cry you mercy;   104
I did not see your Grace. Humbly on my knee
I crave your blessing.

80 mother . . . griefs; *cf. n.*
81 parcell'd: *i.e. distributed among them severally*   general: *i.e.*
    embraces the griefs of all   94 opposite: *in opposition*
103 help: *remedy*

Duch. God bless thee! and put meekness in thy
    breast,
Love, charity, obedience, and true duty.   108

  Rich. Amen; [*Aside.*] and make me die a good old
    man!
That is the butt-end of a mother's blessing;
I marvel that her Grace did leave it out.

  Buck. You cloudy princes and heart-sorrowing
    peers,   112
That bear this heavy mutual load of moan,
Now cheer each other in each other's love:
Though we have spent our harvest of this king,
We are to reap the harvest of his son.   116
The broken rancour of your high-swoll'n hates,
But lately splinter'd, knit, and join'd together,
Must gently be preserv'd, cherish'd, and kept:
Me seemeth good, that, with some little train,   120
Forthwith from Ludlow the young prince be fet
Hither to London, to be crown'd our king.

  Riv. Why with some little train, my Lord of Buck-
    ingham?

  Buck. Marry, my lord, lest by a multitude   124
The new-heal'd wound of malice should break out;
Which would be so much the more dangerous,
By how much the estate is green and yet ungovern'd;
Where every horse bears his commanding rein,   128
And may direct his course as please himself,
As well the fear of harm, as harm apparent,
In my opinion, ought to be prevented.

  Rich. I hope the king made peace with all of us,   132
And the compact is firm and true in me.

112 cloudy: *grief-clouded*
117 broken rancour; *cf. n.*   high-swoll'n: *excessively bitter*
118 splinter'd: *bound up with splints*
120 little train: *few attendants; cf. n.*
121 Ludlow; *cf. n.*   127 estate: *state*   green: *new*
129 please: *may please*

Riv. And so in me; and so, I think, in all:
Yet, since it is but green, it should be put
To no apparent likelihood of breach,   136
Which haply by much company might be urg'd:
Therefore I say with noble Buckingham,
That it is meet so few should fetch the prince.
    Hast. And so say I.   140
    Rich. Then be it so: and go we to determine
Who they shall be that straight shall post to Ludlow.
Madam, and you my sister, will you go
To give your censures in this business?   144
          Exeunt. Mane[n]t Buckingham and Richard.
    Buck. My lord, whoever journeys to the prince,
For God's sake, let not us two stay at home:
For by the way I'll sort occasion,
As index to the story we late talk'd of,   148
To part the queen's proud kindred from the prince.
    Rich. My other self, my counsel's consistory,
My oracle, my prophet! My dear cousin,
I, as a child, will go by thy direction.   152
Towards Ludlow, then, for we'll not stay behind.
                              Exeunt.

Scene Three

[*The Same. A Street*]

*Enter one Citizen at one door and another at
          the other.*

1. *Cit.* Good morrow, neighbour: whither away so
    fast?
2. *Cit.* I promise you, I scarcely know myself:

137 urg'd: *brought on*   144 censures: *opinions*
147 sort: *contrive*   148 index: *introduction, prelude*
149 queen's proud kindred; *cf. n.*
150 consistory: *council-chamber* (*figuratively*)

Hear you the news abroad?

   1. Cit.   Ay; that the king is dead.

   2. Cit. Ill news, by'r lady; seldom comes the bet-
     ter: 4

I fear, I fear, 'twill prove a giddy world.

Enter another Citizen.

   3. Cit. Neighbours, God speed!

   1. Cit.   Give you good morrow, sir.

   3. Cit. Doth the news hold of good King Edward's
     death?

   2. Cit. Ay, sir, it is too true; God help the while! 8

   3. Cit. Then, masters, look to see a troublous world.

   1. Cit. No, no; by God's good grace, his son shall
     reign.

   3. Cit. Woe to that land that's govern'd by a child!

   2. Cit. In him there is a hope of government,   12

Which in his nonage council under him,

And in his full and ripen'd years himself,

No doubt, shall then and till then govern well.

   1. Cit. So stood the state when Henry the Sixth 16

Was crown'd at Paris but at nine months old.

   3. Cit. Stood the state so? no, no, good friends, God
     wot;

For then this land was famously enrich'd

With politic grave counsel; then the king   20

Had virtuous uncles to protect his Grace.

   1. Cit. Why, so hath this, both by his father and
     mother.

   3. Cit. Better it were they all came by his father,

Or by his father there were none at all;   24

For emulation, who shall now be nearest,

4 by'r: *by our (corruption of oath)*   seldom . . . better; *cf. n.*
5 giddy: *confused*   7 hold: *hold good*   9 troublous: *troubled*
11 Woe . . . child; *cf. n.*   13 nonage: *minority*
17 nine months; *cf. n.*   25 emulation: *jealous rivalry*

Will touch us all too near, if God prevent not.
O! full of danger is the Duke of Gloucester,
And the queen's sons and brothers haught and
  proud!   28
And were they to be rul'd, and not to rule,
This sickly land might solace as before.
 1. Cit. Come, come, we fear the worst; all will be
  well.
 3. Cit. When clouds are seen, wise men put on their
  cloaks;   32
When great leaves fall, then winter is at hand;
When the sun sets, who doth not look for night?
Untimely storms make men expect a dearth.
All may be well; but, if God sort it so,   36
'Tis more than we deserve, or I expect.
 2. Cit. Truly, the hearts of men are full of fear:
You cannot reason almost with a man
That looks not heavily and full of dread.   40
 3. Cit. Before the days of change, still is it so:
By a divine instinct men's minds mistrust
Pursuing danger; as, by proof, we see
The waters swell before a boisterous storm.   44
But leave it all to God. Whither away?
 2. Cit. Marry, we were sent for to the justices.
 3. Cit. And so was I: I'll bear you company.
              Exeunt.

28 haught: *haughty*   30 solace: *be happy*
36 sort: *allot*   39 almost: *hardly*
40 That . . . heavily: *who does not look as if aware of the serious day*
43 by: *for*

Scene Four

[*The Same.   A Room in the Palace*]

Enter [*the*] *Archbishop* [*of York, the*] *young* [*Duke of*] *York, the Queen* [*Elizabeth,*] *and the Duchess* [*of York*].

 Arch. Last night, I hear, they lay at Stony-Strat-
  ford;
And at Northampton they do rest to-night:
To-morrow, or next day, they will be here.
 Duch. I long with all my heart to see the prince. 4
I hope he is much grown since last I saw him.
 Q. Eliz. But I hear, no; they say my son of York
Has almost overta'en him in his growth.
 York. Ay, mother, but I would not have it so. 8
 Duch. Why, my good cousin, it is good to grow.
 York. Grandam, one night, as we did sit at supper,
My uncle Rivers talk'd how I did grow
More than my brother: 'Ay,' quoth my uncle Glouces-
  ter, 12
'Small herbs have grace, great weeds do grow apace:'
And since, methinks, I would not grow so fast,
Because sweet flowers are slow and weeds make haste.
 Duch. Good faith, good faith, the saying did not
  hold 16
In him that did object the same to thee:
He was the wretched'st thing when he was young,
So long a-growing, and so leisurely,
That, if his rule were true, he should be gracious. 20
 Arch. And so, no doubt, he is, my gracious madam.
 Duch. I hope he is; but yet let mothers doubt.
 York. Now, by my troth, if I had been remember'd,

1 Stony-Stratford; *cf. n.*   18 wretched'st: *puniest*
23 been remember'd: *recollected*

I could have given my uncle's grace a flout,   24
To touch his growth nearer than he touch'd mine.

  Duch. How, my young York? I prithee, let me
    hear it.

  York. Marry, they say my uncle grew so fast,
That he could gnaw a crust at two hours old: 28
'Twas full two years ere I could get a tooth.
Grandam, this would have been a biting jest.

  Duch. I prithee, pretty York, who told thee this?

  York. Grandam, his nurse.   32

  Duch. His nurse! why, she was dead ere thou wast
    born.

  York. If 'twere not she, I cannot tell who told me.

  Q. Eliz. A parlous boy: go to, you are too shrewd.

  Duch. Good madam, be not angry with the child. 36

  Q. Eliz. Pitchers have ears.

Enter a Messenger.

  Arch. Here comes a messenger. What news?

  Mess. Such news, my lord, as grieves me to report.

  Q. Eliz. How doth the prince?

  Mess.   Well, madam, and in health. 40

  Duch. What is thy news?

  Mess. Lord Rivers and Lord Grey are sent to Pom-
    fret,
With them Sir Thomas Vaughan, prisoners.

  Duch. Who hath committed them?

  Mess.   The mighty dukes, 44
Gloucester and Buckingham.

  Arch.   For what offence?

  Mess. The sum of all I can I have disclos'd:
Why, or for what, the nobles were committed
Is all unknown to me, my gracious lord.   48

28 *Cf. n.*   35 parlous: *clever, keen*
37 Pitchers; *cf. n.*   S. d. *Cf. n.*

Q. Eliz. Ay me! I see the ruin of my house!
The tiger now hath seiz'd the gentle hind;
Insulting tyranny begins to jut
Upon the innocent and aweless throne: 52
Welcome destruction, blood, and massacre!
I see, as in a map, the end of all.

    Duch. Accursed and unquiet wrangling days,
How many of you have mine eyes beheld!   56
My husband lost his life to get the crown,
And often up and down my sons were toss'd
For me to joy and weep their gain and loss.
And being seated, and domestic broils   60
Clean over-blown, themselves, the conquerors,
Make war upon themselves; brother to brother,
Blood to blood, self against self: O preposterous
And frantic outrage, end thy damned spleen;   64
Or let me die, to look on earth no more!

    Q. Eliz. Come, come, my boy; we will to sanctuary.
Madam, farewell.

    Duch.   Stay, I will go with you.

    Q. Eliz. You have no cause.

    Arch. [*To the Queen.*] My gracious lady, go;   68
And thither bear your treasure and your goods.
For my part, I'll resign unto your Grace
The seal I keep: and so betide to me
As well I tender you and all of yours!   72
Go; I'll conduct you to the sanctuary.   *Exeunt.*

---

50 hind: *doe*   51 jut: *encroach*
52 aweless: *i.e. because occupied by a young prince*
54 map; *cf. n.*   66 sanctuary; *cf. n.*

ACT THIRD

Scene One

[*The Same.   A Street*]

The Trumpets sound.   Enter young Prince [of Wales], the Dukes of Gloucester and Buckingham, Lord Cardinal [Bourchier, Catesby], with Others.

> *Buck.* Welcome, sweet prince, to London, to your chamber.
>
> *Rich.* Welcome, dear cousin, my thoughts' sovereign;

The weary way hath made you melancholy.

> *Prince.* No, uncle; but our crosses on the way   4

Have made it tedious, wearisome, and heavy:

I want more uncles here to welcome me.

> *Rich.* Sweet prince, the untainted virtue of your years

Hath not yet div'd into the world's deceit: 8

No more can you distinguish of a man

Than of his outward show; which, God he knows,

Seldom or never jumpeth with the heart.

Those uncles which you want were dangerous;   12

Your Grace attended to their sugar'd words,

But look'd not on the poison of their hearts:

God keep you from them, and from such false friends!

> *Prince.* God keep me from false friends! but they were none.   16
>
> *Rich.* My lord, the Mayor of London comes to greet you.

Scene One S. d. Cardinal; *cf. n.*   1 chamber: *royal residence*
4 crosses: *vexations*   11 jumpeth: *agrees*
16 *Cf. n.*

Enter [the] Lord Mayor [and his Train].

L. May. God bless your Grace with health and
happy days!

Prince. I thank you, good my lord; and thank you
all.

I thought my mother and my brother York   20
Would long ere this have met us on the way:
Fie! what a slug is Hastings, that he comes not
To tell us whether they will come or no.

Enter Lord Hastings.

Buck. And in good time here comes the sweating
lord.   24

Prince. Welcome, my lord. What, will our mother
come?

Hast. On what occasion, God he knows, not I,
The queen your mother, and your brother York,
Have taken sanctuary: the tender prince   28
Would fain have come with me to meet your Grace,
But by his mother was perforce withheld.

Buck. Fie! what an indirect and peevish course
Is this of hers! Lord Cardinal, will your Grace   32
Persuade the queen to send the Duke of York
Unto his princely brother presently?
If she deny, Lord Hastings, go with him,
And from her jealous arms pluck him perforce.   36

Card. My Lord of Buckingham, if my weak oratory
Can from his mother win the Duke of York,
Anon expect him here; but if she be obdurate
To mild entreaties, God [in heaven] forbid   40
We should infringe the holy privilege
Of blessed sanctuary! not for all this land

17 S. d. *Cf. n.*   22 slug: *sluggard*
30 perforce: *by force*   36 pluck him; *cf. n.*
39 Anon: *soon*   40, 41 God . . . infringe; *cf. n.*

Would I be guilty of so great a sin.

    Buck. You are too senseless-obstinate, my lord,   44
Too ceremonious and traditional:
Weigh it but with the grossness of this age,
You break not sanctuary in seizing him.
The benefit thereof is always granted   48
To those whose dealings have deserv'd the place
And those who have the wit to claim the place:
This prince hath neither claim'd it, nor deserv'd it;
And therefore, in mine opinion, cannot have it: 52
Then, taking him from thence that is not there,
You break no privilege nor charter there.
Oft have I heard of sanctuary men,
But sanctuary children ne'er till now.   56

    Card. My lord, you shall o'er-rule my mind for once.
Come on, Lord Hastings, will you go with me?

    Hast. I go, my lord.

    Prince. Good lords, make all the speedy haste you
       may.   60

                 Exeunt Cardinal and Hastings.
Say, uncle Gloucester, if our brother come,
Where shall we sojourn till our coronation?

    Rich. Where it think'st best unto your royal self.
If I may counsel you, some day or two   64
Your highness shall repose you at the Tower:
Then where you please, and shall be thought most fit
For your best health and recreation.

    Prince. I do not like the Tower, of any place: 68
Did Julius Cæsar build that place, my lord?

    Buck. He did, my gracious lord, begin that place,

---

44 senseless-obstinate: *obstinate without reason*
45 Too . . . traditional: *too given to standing on ceremony and
precedent*   46 grossness: *lack of nicety; cf. n.*
53 taking . . . there: *i.e. because, actually, he is not in sanctuary*
56 children; *cf. n.*   64 some: *a*
65 the Tower; *cf. n.*   68 of any place: *most of all places*
69 Julius Cæsar; *cf. n.*

Which, since, succeeding ages have re-edified.

    Prince. Is it upon record, or else reported   72
Successively from age to age, he built it?

    Buck. Upon record, my gracious lord.

    Prince. But say, my lord, it were not register'd,
Methinks the truth should live from age to age,   76
As 'twere retail'd to all posterity,
Even to the general [all-]ending day.

    Rich. [*Aside.*] So wise so young, they say, do never
      live long.

    Prince. What say you, uncle?   80

    Rich. I say, without characters, fame lives long.
[*Aside.*] Thus, like the formal Vice, Iniquity,
I moralize two meanings in one word.

    Prince. That Julius Cæsar was a famous man;   84
With what his valour did enrich his wit,
His wit set down to make his valour live:
Death makes no conquest of his conqueror,
For now he lives in fame, though not in life.   88
I'll tell you what, my cousin Buckingham,—

    Buck. What, my gracious lord?

    Prince. An if I live until I be a man,
I'll win our ancient right in France again,   92
Or die a soldier, as I liv'd a king.

    Rich. [*Aside.*] Short summers lightly have a for-
      ward spring.

      Enter young York, Hastings, and Cardinal.

    Buck. Now, in good time, here comes the Duke of
      York.

    Prince. Richard of York! how fares our noble
      brother?   96

77 retail'd: *handed down*   78 [all-]ending day: *i.e. doomsday*
79 So . . . long; *cf. n.*   81 characters: *written documents*
82 Vice, Iniquity; *cf. n.*   83 moralize: *interpret*
85 With what: *that with which*   94 lightly: *commonly*

York. Well, my dear lord; so must I call you now.

Prince. Ay, brother, to our grief, as it is yours:
Too late he died that might have kept that title,
Which by his death hath lost much majesty.   100

Rich. How fares our cousin, noble Lord of York?

York. I thank you, gentle uncle. O, my lord,
You said that idle weeds are fast in growth:
The prince my brother hath outgrown me far.   104

Rich. He hath, my lord.

York.   And therefore is he idle?

Rich. O, my fair cousin, I must not say so.

York. Then he is more beholding to you than I.

Rich. He may command me as my sovereign;   108
But you have power in me as in a kinsman.

York. I pray you, uncle, give me this dagger.

Rich. My dagger, little cousin? with all my heart.

Prince. A beggar, brother?   112

York. Of my kind uncle, that I know will give;
And, being but a toy, which is no grief to give.

Rich. A greater gift than that I'll give my cousin.

York. A greater gift! O, that's the sword to it.   116

Rich. Ay, gentle cousin, were it light enough.

York. O, then, I see, you'll part but with light gifts;
In weightier things you'll say a beggar nay.

Rich. It is too weighty for your Grace to wear.   120

York. I weigh it lightly, were it heavier.

Rich. What! would you have my weapon, little lord?

York. I would, that I might thank you, as you call
    me.

Rich. How?   124

York. Little.

Prince. My Lord of York will still be cross in talk.
Uncle, your Grace knows how to bear with him.

97 dear; *cf. n.*   99 late: *lately*
114 toy: *trifle*   126 cross: *given to opposition*

York. You mean, to bear me, not to bear with me: 128
Uncle, my brother mocks both you and me.
Because that I am little, like an ape,
He thinks that you should bear me on your shoulders.

    Buck. With what a sharp provided wit he rea-
        sons!   132
To mitigate the scorn he gives his uncle,
He prettily and aptly taunts himself:
So cunning and so young is wonderful.

    Rich. My lord, will 't please you pass along?   136
Myself and my good cousin Buckingham
Will to your mother, to entreat of her
To meet you at the Tower and welcome you.

    York. What! will you go unto the Tower, my
        lord?   140

    Prince. My Lord Protector will have it so.

    York. I shall not sleep in quiet at the Tower.

    Rich. Why, what should you fear?

    York. Marry, my uncle Clarence' angry ghost: 144
My grandam told me he was murther'd there.

    Prince. I fear no uncles dead.

    Rich. Nor none that live, I hope.

    Prince. An if they live, I hope, I need not fear.   148
But come, my lord; and, with a heavy heart,
Thinking on them, go I unto the Tower.

                A Sennet. Exeunt Prince, York,
                       Hastings, and Dorset.
      Mane[n]t Richard, Buckingham, and Catesby.

    Buck. Think you, my lord, this little prating York
Was not incensed by his subtle mother   152
To taunt and scorn you thus opprobriously?

    Rich. No doubt, no doubt: O! 'tis a perilous boy;

---

131 shoulders; *cf. n.*   132 provided: *ready*
133 scorn: *taunt*   141 *Cf. n.*
150 on: *of*   S. d. Sennet; *cf. n.*   152 incensed: *instigated*
154 perilous: *i.e. parlous*

Bold, quick, ingenious, forward, capable:

He's all the mother's, from the top to toe.   156

    Buck. Well, let them rest. Come hither, Catesby;
      thou art sworn

As deeply to effect what we intend

As closely to conceal what we impart.

Thou know'st our reasons urg'd upon the way: 160

What think'st thou? is it not an easy matter

To make William Lord Hastings of our mind,

For the instalment of this noble duke

In the seat royal of this famous isle?   164

    Cate. He for his father's sake so loves the prince

That he will not be won to aught against him.

    Buck. What think'st thou, then, of Stanley? will
      not he?

    Cate. He will do all in all as Hastings doth.   168

    Buck. Well then, no more but this: go, gentle
      Catesby,

And, as it were far off, sound thou Lord Hastings,

How he doth stand affected to our purpose;

And summon him to-morrow to the Tower,   172

To sit about the coronation.

If thou dost find him tractable to us,

Encourage him, and tell him all our reasons:

If he be leaden, icy-cold, unwilling,   176

Be thou so too, and so break off the talk,

And give us notice of his inclination;

For we to-morrow hold divided councils,

Wherein thyself shalt highly be employ'd.   180

    Rich. Commend me to Lord William: tell him,
      Catesby,

His ancient knot of dangerous adversaries

155 forward: *precocious*   capable: *intelligent*
164 seat royal: *royal throne*   170 far off: *indirectly; cf. n.*
173 sit: *confer*   182 knot: *group*

To-morrow are let blood at Pomfret Castle;
And bid my lord, for joy of this good news,   184
Give Mistress Shore one gentle kiss the more.

Buck. Good Catesby, go, effect this business soundly.
Cate. My good lords both, with all the heed I can.
Rich. Shall we hear from you, Catesby, ere we
    sleep?   188
Cate. You shall, my lord.
Rich. At Crosby House, there shall you find us both.
                                            Exit Catesby.
Buck. Now, my lord, what shall we do if we per-
    ceive
Lord Hastings will not yield to our complots?   192
Rich. Chop off his head; something we will deter-
    mine:
And, look, when I am king, claim thou of me
The earldom of Hereford, and all the moveables
Whereof the king my brother was possess'd.   196
Buck. I'll claim that promise at your Grace's hand.
Rich. And look to have it yielded with all kindness.
Come, let us sup betimes, that afterwards
We may digest our complots in some form.   200
                                            Exeunt.

Scene Two

[*The Same.   Before Lord Hastings' House*]

Enter a Messenger to the door of Hastings.

Mess. [*Knocking.*] My lord! my lord!
Hast. [*Within.*] Who knocks?
Mess. One from the Lord Stanley.
Hast. [*Within.*] What is 't o'clock?   4

---

185 Mistress Shore; *cf. n.*   192 complots: *plots, conspiracies*
195, 196 *Cf. n.*   195 moveables: *personal property*

Mess. Upon the stroke of four.

Enter Lord Hastings.

Hast. Cannot my Lord Stanley sleep these tedious
   nights?

Mess. So it appears by that I have to say.
First, he commends him to your noble self.   8

Hast. What then?

Mess. Then certifies your lordship, that this night
He dreamt the boar had rased off his helm:
Besides, he says there are two councils kept;   12
And that may be determin'd at the one
Which may make you and him to rue at th' other.
Therefore he sends to know your lordship's pleasure,
If you will presently take horse with him,   16
And with all speed post with him toward the north,
To shun the danger that his soul divines.

Hast. Go, fellow, go, return unto thy lord;
Bid him not fear the separated council: 20
His honour and myself are at the one,
And at the other is my good friend Catesby;
Where nothing can proceed that toucheth us
Whereof I shall not have intelligence.   24
Tell him his fears are shallow, without instance:
And for his dreams, I wonder he's so simple
To trust the mockery of unquiet slumbers.
To fly the boar before the boar pursues,   28
Were to incense the boar to follow us
And make pursuit where he did mean no chase.
Go, bid thy master rise and come to me;
And we will both together to the Tower,   32
Where, he shall see, the boar will use us kindly.

5 stroke of four; *cf. n.*   10 certifies: *informs*
11 boar: *i.e. Richard*   rased: *torn*
20 separated council; *cf. n.*   25 instance: *cause, motive*
26 his dreams; *cf. n.*   27 To: *as to*

Mess. I'll go, my lord, and tell him what you say.
                                                    Exit.

                        Enter Catesby.

Cate. Many good morrows to my noble lord!
Hast. Good morrow, Catesby; you are early stir-
    ring.   36
What news, what news, in this our tottering state?
Cate. It is a reeling world, indeed, my lord;
And I believe will never stand upright
Till Richard wear the garland of the realm.   40
Hast. How! wear the garland! dost thou mean the
    crown?
Cate. Ay, my good lord.
Hast. I'll have this crown of mine cut from my
    shoulders
Before I'll see the crown so foul misplac'd.   44
But canst thou guess that he doth aim at it?
Cate. Ay, on my life; and hopes to find you forward
Upon his party for the gain thereof:
And thereupon he sends you this good news,   48
That this same very day your enemies,
The kindred of the queen, must die at Pomfret.
Hast. Indeed, I am no mourner for that news,
Because they have been still my adversaries;   52
But that I'll give my voice on Richard's side,
To bar my master's heirs in true descent,
God knows I will not do it, to the death.
Cate. God keep your lordship in that gracious
    mind!   56
Hast. But I shall laugh at this a twelve-month
    hence,
That they which brought me in my master's hate,

43 crown: *head*   52 still: *always*
55 to the death: *i.e. even if my refusal cost me my life*

I live to look upon their tragedy.
Well, Catesby, ere a fortnight make me older,   60
I'll send some packing that yet think not on 't.

Cate. 'Tis a vile thing to die, my gracious lord,
When men are unprepar'd and look not for it.

Hast. O monstrous, monstrous! and so falls it out 64
With Rivers, Vaughan, Grey; and so 'twill do
With some men else, that think themselves as safe
As thou and I; who, as thou know'st, are dear
To princely Richard and to Buckingham.   68

Cate. The princes both make high account of you;
[*Aside.*] For they account his head upon the bridge.

Hast. I know they do, and I have well deserv'd it.

Enter Lord Stanley.

Come on, come on; where is your boar-spear, man? 72
Fear you the boar, and go so unprovided?

Stan. My lord, good morrow; good morrow, Catesby:
You may jest on, but by the holy rood,
I do not like these several councils, I.   76

Hast. My lord, I hold my life as dear as yours;
And never, in my days, I do protest,
Was it so precious to me as 'tis now.
Think you, but that I know our state secure,   80
I would be so triumphant as I am?

Stan. The lords at Pomfret, when they rode from
    London,
Were jocund and suppos'd their states were sure,
And they indeed had no cause to mistrust;   84
But yet you see how soon the day o'ercast.
This sudden stab of rancour I misdoubt;
Pray God, I say, I prove a needless coward!

70 head . . . bridge: *cf. n.*   75 rood: *cross*
83 jocund: *carefree, merry*   sure: *secure*
85 o'ercast: *became overcast*   86 misdoubt: *suspect*
87 needless: *without cause or reason*

What, shall we toward the Tower? the day is spent. 88
  Hast. Come, come, have with you. Wot you what,
    my lord?
To-day the lords you talk of are beheaded.
  Stan. They, for their truth, might better wear their
    heads,
Than some that have accus'd them wear their hats. 92
But come, my lord, let's away.

          Enter a Pursuivant.

  Hast. Go on before; I'll talk with this good fellow.
            Exeunt Lord Stanley and Catesby.
How now, sirrah! how goes the world with thee?
  Purs. The better that your lordship please to ask. 96
  Hast. I tell thee, man, 'tis better with me now
Than when thou met'st me last where now we meet:
Then was I going prisoner to the Tower,
By the suggestion of the queen's allies; 100
But now, I tell thee,—keep it to thyself,—
This day those enemies are put to death,
And I in better state than e'er I was.
  Purs. God hold it to your honour's good content! 104
  Hast. Gramercy, fellow: there, drink that for me.
              Throws him his purse.
  Purs. I thank your honour.   *Exit Pursuivant.*

           Enter a Priest.

  Pr. Well met, my lord; I am glad to see your honour.
  Hast. I thank thee, good Sir John, with all my
    heart. 108
I am in your debt for your last exercise;

88 spent; *cf. n.*
89 have with you: *I will go with you*   Wot: *know*
93 S. d. Pursuivant: *junior officer attending on a herald*
98 now we meet; *cf. n.*   100 suggestion: *urging (in a bad sense)*
105 Gramercy: *thanks*   108 Sir John; *cf. n.*
109 exercise: *act of worship, discourse*

Come the next Sabbath, and I will content you.
  Pr. I'll wait upon your lordship.

Enter Buckingham.

  Buck. What, talking with a priest, lord chamber-
    lain?   112
Your friends at Pomfret, they do need the priest:
Your honour hath no shriving work in hand.
  Hast. Good faith, and when I met this holy man,
The men you talk of came into my mind.   116
What, go you toward the Tower?
  Buck. I do, my lord; but long I cannot stay there:
I shall return before your lordship thence.
  Hast. Nay, like enough, for I stay dinner there. 120
  Buck. [*Aside.*] And supper too, although thou
    know'st it not.
Come, will you go?
  Hast.   I'll wait upon your lordship.
                         Exeunt.

Scene Three

[*Pomfret. Before the Castle*]

*Enter Sir Richard Ratcliff, with Halberds, carrying
  the nobles [Rivers, Grey, and Vaughan] to death at
  Pomfret.*

  Riv. Sir Richard Ratcliff, let me tell thee this:
To-day shalt thou behold a subject die
For truth, for duty, and for loyalty.
  Grey. God bless the prince from all the pack of
    you!   4
A knot you are of damned blood-suckers.

112 talking; *cf. n.*   114 shriving; *cf. n.*
Scene Three S. d. *Cf. n.*

Vaugh. You live that shall cry woe for this hereafter!

Rat. Dispatch; the limit of your lives is out.

Riv. O Pomfret, Pomfret! O thou bloody prison! 8
Fatal and ominous to noble peers!
Within the guilty closure of thy walls
Richard the Second here was hack'd to death;
And, for more slander to thy dismal seat,   12
We give to thee our guiltless blood to drink.

Grey. Now Margaret's curse is fall'n upon our
heads,
When she exclaim'd on Hastings, you, and I,
For standing by when Richard stabb'd her son.   16

Riv. Then curs'd she Richard, then curs'd she
Buckingham,
Then curs'd she Hastings: O! remember, God,
To hear her prayer for them, as now for us;
And for my sister and her princely sons,   20
Be satisfied, dear God, with our true blood,
Which, as thou know'st, unjustly must be spilt.

Rat. Make haste; the hour of death is expiate.

Riv. Come, Grey, come, Vaughan; let us here em-
brace.   24
Farewell until we meet again in heaven.

Exeunt.

7 out: *at an end*   10 closure: *enclosure*
11 *Cf. n*   14 Margaret's curse; *cf. n.*
23 expiate: *fully come*

Scene Four

[*London.　The Tower*]

Enter Buckingham, Derby, Hastings, Bishop of Ely,
　Norfolk, Ratcliff, Lovel, with others, at a Table.

　Hast. Now noble peers, the cause why we are met
Is to determine of the coronation:
In God's name, speak, when is the royal day?
　Buck. Is all things ready for the royal time?　　4
　Der. It is; and wants but nomination.
　Ely. To-morrow then I judge a happy day.
　Buck. Who knows the Lord Protector's mind herein?
Who is most inward with the noble duke?　　8
　Ely. Your Grace, we think, should soonest know his
　　mind.
　Buck. We know each other's faces; for our hearts,
He knows no more of mine than I of yours;
Nor I of his, my lord, than you of mine.　　12
Lord Hastings, you and he are near in love.
　Hast. I thank his Grace, I know he loves me well;
But, for his purpose in the coronation,
I have not sounded him, nor he deliver'd　　16
His gracious pleasure any way therein:
But you, my honourable lords, may name the time;
And in the duke's behalf I'll give my voice,
Which, I presume, he'll take in gentle part.　　20

Enter Richard.

　Ely. In happy time, here comes the duke himself.
　Rich. My noble lords and cousins all, good morrow.
I have been long a sleeper; but, I trust,
My absence doth neglect no great design,　　24

Scene Four S. d. Derby: *i.e. Stanley*　　　5 nomination: *appointing*
6 happy: *suitable*　　　　　　　　　　　8 inward: *familiar, intimate*
9 should soonest: *is most likely to*　　　21 In happy time: *opportunely*

Which by my presence might have been concluded.

   Buck. Had you not come upon your cue, my lord,
William Lord Hastings had pronounc'd your part,
I mean, your voice, for crowning of the king.   28

   Rich. Than my Lord Hastings no man might be
     bolder:
His lordship knows me well, and loves me well.
My Lord of Ely, when I was last in Holborn,
I saw good strawberries in your garden there;   32
I do beseech you send for some of them.

   Ely. Marry, and will, my lord, with all my heart.

                             Exit Bishop.

   Rich. Cousin of Buckingham, a word with you.

                          [Takes him aside.]

Catesby hath sounded Hastings in our business,   36
And finds the testy gentleman so hot,
That he will lose his head ere give consent
His master's child, as worshipfully he terms it,
Shall lose the royalty of England's throne.   40

   Buck. Withdraw yourself a while; I'll go with you.

               Exeunt [Richard and Buckingham].

   Der. We have not yet set down this day of triumph.
To-morrow, in my judgment, is too sudden;
For I myself am not so well provided   44
As else I would be, were the day prolong'd.

       [Re-]enter the Bishop of Ely.

   Ely. Where is my lord, the Duke of Gloucester?
I have sent for these strawberries.

   Hast. His Grace looks cheerfully and smooth this
     morning: 48
There's some conceit or other likes him well,

26 upon: *at*   cue; *cf. n.*   28 voice: *vote*
32 good strawberries; *cf. n.*   37 testy: *quick-tempered*
45 prolong'd: *postponed*
49 conceit: *idea, thought*   likes: *that pleases*

When that he bids good morrow with such spirit.
I think there's never a man in Christendom
Can lesser hide his love or hate than he;   52
For by his face straight shall you know his heart.

   Der. What of his heart perceive you in his face
By any livelihood he show'd to-day?

   Hast. Marry, that with no man here he is of-
    fended;   56
For, were he, he had shown it in his looks.

   [*Der.* I pray God he be not, I say.]

    [*Re-*]*enter Richard and Buckingham.*

   Rich. I pray you all, tell me what they deserve
That do conspire my death with devilish plots   60
Of damned witchcraft, and that have prevail'd
Upon my body with their hellish charms?

   Hast. The tender love I bear your Grace, my lord,
Makes me most forward in this princely presence   64
To doom th' offenders, whosoe'er they be:
I say, my lord, they have deserved death.

   Rich. Then be your eyes the witness of their evil.
Look how I am bewitch'd; behold mine arm   68
Is like a blasted sapling, wither'd up:
And this is Edward's wife, that monstrous witch,
Consorted with that harlot strumpet Shore,
That by their witchcraft thus have marked me.   72

   Hast. If they have done this deed, my noble lord,—

   Rich. If! thou protector of this damned strumpet,
Talk'st thou to me of ifs? Thou art a traitor:
Off with his head! now, by Saint Paul, I swear,   76
I will not dine until I see the same.
Lovel and Ratcliff, look that it be done:

---

55 livelihood: *animated appearance*
61 prevail'd: *effected harm*
71 Consorted: *associated*

58 S. d. *Cf. n.*
69 blasted sapling; *cf. n.*
74 If; *cf. n.*

The rest, that love me, rise, and follow me.

> *Exeunt.   Mane[n]t Lovel and Ratcliff,*
> *with the Lord Hastings.*

Hast. Woe, woe, for England! not a whit for me;   80
For I, too fond, might have prevented this.
Stanley did dream the boar did rase our helms;
And I did scorn it, and disdain to fly.
Three times to-day my foot-cloth horse did stumble,   84
And started when he look'd upon the Tower,
As loath to bear me to the slaughter-house.
O! now I need the priest that spake to me:
I now repent I told the pursuivant,   88
As too triumphing, how mine enemies
To-day at Pomfret bloodily were butcher'd
And I myself secure in grace and favour.
O Margaret, Margaret! now thy heavy curse   92
Is lighted on poor Hastings' wretched head.

Rat. Come, come, dispatch; the duke would be at
    dinner:
Make a short shrift, he longs to see your head.

Hast. O momentary grace of mortal men,   96
Which we more hunt for than the grace of God!
Who builds his hope in air of your good looks,
Lives like a drunken sailor on a mast;
Ready with every nod to tumble down   100
Into the fatal bowels of the deep.

Lov. Come, come, dispatch; 'tis bootless to exclaim.

Hast. O bloody Richard! miserable England!
I prophesy the fearfull'st time to thee   104
That ever wretched age hath look'd upon.
Come, lead me to the block; bear him my head:

81 fond: *foolish*   84 foot-cloth; *cf. n.*
95 shrift: *confession*   98 air . . . looks; *cf. n.*
99 drunken . . . mast; *cf. n.*   102 bootless: *useless*

They smile at me who shortly shall be dead.

Exeunt.

Scene Five

[London.   The Tower Walls]

Enter Richard and Buckingham, in rotten
armour, marvellous ill-favoured.

Rich. Come, cousin, canst thou quake, and change
 thy colour,
Murther thy breath in middle of a word,
And then again begin, and stop again,
As if thou wert distraught and mad with terror? 4
 Buck. Tut! I can counterfeit the deep tragedian,
Speak and look back, and pry on every side,
Tremble and start at wagging of a straw,
Intending deep suspicion: ghastly looks   8
Are at my service, like enforced smiles;
And both are ready in their offices,
At any time, to grace my stratagems.
But what! is Catesby gone?   12
 Rich. He is; and, see, he brings the mayor along.

Enter the [Lord] Mayor and Catesby.

 Buck. Lord Mayor,—
 Rich. Look to the drawbridge there!
 Buck.   Hark! a drum.
 Rich. Catesby, o'erlook the walls.   16
 Buck. Lord Mayor, the reason we have sent,—
 Rich. Look back, defend thee; here are enemies.
 Buck. God and our innocency defend and guard us!

Scene Five S. d. rotten: *rusty*   4 distraught: *mentally deranged*
8 Intending: *pretending*

Enter Lovel and Ratcliff, with Hastings' head.

Rich. Be patient, they are friends, Ratcliff and
    Lovel.   20
Lov. Here is the head of that ignoble traitor,
The dangerous and unsuspected Hastings.
Rich. So dear I lov'd the man that I must weep.
I took him for the plainest harmless creature   24
That breath'd upon the earth a Christian;
Made him my book, wherein my soul recorded
The history of all her secret thoughts:
So smooth he daub'd his vice with show of virtue,   28
That, his apparent open guilt omitted,
I mean his conversation with Shore's wife,
He liv'd from all attainder of suspects.
   Buck. Well, well, he was the covert'st shelter'd
    traitor   32
That ever liv'd.
Would you imagine, or almost believe,—
Were 't not that by great preservation
We live to tell it,—that the subtle traitor   36
This day had plotted, in the council-house,
To murther me and my good Lord of Gloucester?
   May. Had he done so?
   Rich. What! think you we are Turks or infidels? 40
Or that we would, against the form of law,
Proceed thus rashly in the villain's death,
But that the extreme peril of the case,
The peace of England and our person's safety,   44
Enforc'd us to this execution?
   May. Now, fair befall you! he deserv'd his death;
And your good Graces both have well proceeded,

---

28 daub'd: *glossed*   30 conversation: *criminal conversation*
31 from: *free from*   attainder of suspects: *stain of suspicions*
32 covert'st: *most secret*   34 almost: *even*
40 Turks; *cf. n.*   46 fair befall: *good fortune attend*

To warn false traitors from the like attempts.   48
  Buck. I never look'd for better at his hands,
After he once fell in with Mistress Shore.
Yet had we not determin'd he should die,
Until your lordship came to see his end;   52
Which now the loving haste of these our friends,
Something against our meanings, have prevented:
Because, my lord, I would have had you heard
The traitor speak, and timorously confess   56
The manner and the purpose of his treasons;
That you might well have signified the same
Unto the citizens, who haply may
Misconster us in him, and wail his death.   60
  May. But, my good lord, your Grace's words shall
    serve,
As well as I had seen and heard him speak:
And do not doubt, right noble princes both,
But I'll acquaint our duteous citizens   64
With all your just proceedings in this case.
  Rich. And to that end we wish'd your lordship here,
T' avoid the censures of the carping world.
  Buck. Which since you come too late of our intent, 68
Yet witness what you hear we did intend:
And so, my good Lord Mayor, we bid farewell.
                    Exit [*Lord*] *Mayor.*
  Rich. Go, after, after, cousin Buckingham.
The mayor towards Guildhall hies him in all post: 72
There, at your meetest vantage of the time,
Infer the bastardy of Edward's children:
Tell them how Edward put to death a citizen,
Only for saying he would make his son   76
Heir to the crown; meaning indeed his house,

49, 50 *Cf. n.*   55 heard: *to have heard*
60 Misconster: *misconstrue*   64 duteous: *dutiful*
67 carping: *fault-finding*   68 of our intent; *cf. n.*
72 post: *haste*   73 meetest vantage: *most favorable opportunity*
75 a citizen; *cf. n.*

Which by the sign thereof was termed so.
Moreover, urge his hateful luxury
And bestial appetite in change of lust;   80
Which stretch'd unto their servants, daughters, wives,
Even where his raging eye or savage heart
Without control lusted to make a prey.
Nay, for a need, thus far come near my person: 84
Tell them, when that my mother went with child
Of that insatiate Edward, noble York,
My princely father, then had wars in France;
And, by true computation of the time,   88
Found that the issue was not his begot;
Which well appeared in his lineaments,
Being nothing like the noble duke my father.
Yet touch this sparingly, as 'twere far off,   92
Because, my lord, you know my mother lives.
   Buck. Doubt not, my lord, I'll play the orator
As if the golden fee for which I plead
Were for myself: and so, my lord, adieu.   96
   Rich. If you thrive well, bring them to Baynard's
      Castle;
Where you shall find me well accompanied
With reverend fathers and well-learned bishops.
   Buck. I go; and towards three or four o'clock   100
Look for the news that the Guildhall affords.
                                   Exit Buckingham.
   Rich. Go, Lovel, with all speed to Doctor Shaw;
[*To Catesby.*] Go thou to Friar Penker; bid them both
Meet me within this hour at Baynard's Castle.   104
                        Exit [*Catesby, with Lovel*].
Now will I go to take some privy order,

78 sign; *cf. n.*   79 luxury: *lechery*
84 for a need: *if necessary*   thus . . . near; *cf. n.*
90 Which: *a fact which*   well appeared: *was clearly apparent*
97 Baynard's Castle; *cf. n.*   102 Doctor Shaw; *cf. n.*
103 Friar Penker; *cf. n.*   105 privy order: *private measures*

To draw the brats of Clarence out of sight;
And to give order that no manner person
Have any time recourse unto the princes.   108
                Exeunt [Richard and Ratcliff].

Scene Six

[The Same. A Street]

Enter a Scrivener.

  Scriv. Here is the indictment of the good Lord
    Hastings;
Which in a set hand fairly is engross'd,
That it may be to-day read o'er in Paul's:
And mark how well the sequel hangs together.   4
Eleven hours I have spent to write it over,
For yesternight by Catesby was it sent me.
The precedent was full as long a-doing;
And yet within these five hours Hastings liv'd,   8
Untainted, unexamin'd, free, at liberty.
Here's a good world the while! Who is so gross
That cannot see this palpable device?
Yet who so bold but says he sees it not?   12
Bad is the world; and all will come to naught,
When such ill dealing must be seen in thought.

                        Exit.

107 manner: *manner of*   108 recourse: *access*
Scene Six S. d. Scrivener: *professional scribe*
2 engross'd: *written out in a legal hand*
7 precedent: *original rough copy*
9 Untainted: *without suspicion of guilt*   10 gross: *stupid*
14 seen in thought: *i.e. observed but not referred to*

Scene Seven

[*The Same.   The Court of Baynard's Castle*]

Enter Richard and Buckingham at several doors.

Rich. How now, how now! what say the citizens?
Buck. Now, by the holy mother of our Lord,
The citizens are mum, say not a word.
    Rich. Touch'd you the bastardy of Edward's chil-
      dren?   4
    Buck. I did; with his contract with Lady Lucy,
And his contract by deputy in France;
Th' unsatiate greediness of his desire,
And his enforcement of the city wives;   8
His tyranny for trifles; his own bastardy,
As being got, your father then in France,
And his resemblance being not like the duke:
Withal I did infer your lineaments,   12
Being the right idea of your father,
Both in your form and nobleness of mind;
Laid open all your victories in Scotland,
Your discipline in war, wisdom in peace,   16
Your bounty, virtue, fair humility;
Indeed, left nothing fitting for your purpose
Untouch'd or slightly handled in discourse;
And when my oratory drew toward end,   20
I bid them that did love their country's good
Cry 'God save Richard, England's royal king!'
    Rich. And did they so?
    Buck. No, so God help me, they spake not a
      word;   24
But, like dumb statues or breathing stones,

---

5 Lady Lucy; *cf. n.*   6 contract by deputy; *cf. n.*
11 resemblance: *appearance*   13 right idea: *exact image*
15 victories; *cf. n.*   25 statues: *a trisyllable here; cf. n.*

Star'd each on other, and look'd deadly pale.
Which when I saw, I reprehended them;
And ask'd the mayor what meant this wilful silence: 28
His answer was, the people were not us'd
To be spoke to but by the recorder.
Then he was urg'd to tell my tale again:
'Thus saith the duke, thus hath the duke inferr'd;'   32
But nothing spoke in warrant from himself.
When he had done, some followers of mine own,
At lower end of the hall, hurl'd up their caps,
And some ten voices cried, 'God save King Richard!'   36
And thus I took the vantage of those few,
'Thanks, gentle citizens and friends,' quoth I;
'This general applause and cheerful shout
Argues your wisdom and your love to Richard:'   40
And even here brake off, and came away.
   Rich. What tongueless blocks were they! would they
     not speak?
Will not the mayor, then, and his brethren come?
   Buck. The mayor is here at hand. Intend some
     fear;   44
Be not you spoke with but by mighty suit:
And look you get a prayer-book in your hand,
And stand between two churchmen, good my lord:
For on that ground I'll make a holy descant: 48
And be not easily won to our requests;
Play the maid's part, still answer nay, and take it.
   Rich. I go; and if you plead as well for them
As I can say nay to thee for myself,   52
No doubt we bring it to a happy issue.
   Buck. Go, go, up to the leads! the Lord Mayor
     knocks.   [*Exit Richard.*]

30 recorder: *a city official*
38 quoth: *said*
44–245 Cf. n.
50 maid's part; *cf. n.*
37 vantage: *advantage*
40 Argues: *shows*
45 by mighty suit: *after urgent entreaty*

Enter the [Lord] Mayor, [Aldermen,] and Citizens.

Welcome, my lord: I dance attendance here;
I think the duke will not be spoke withal.   56

       Enter [from the Castle,] Catesby.

Now, Catesby! what says your lord to my request?
  Cate. He doth entreat your Grace, my noble lord,
To visit him to-morrow or next day.
He is within, with two right reverend fathers,   60
Divinely bent to meditation;
And in no worldly suits would he be mov'd,
To draw him from his holy exercise.
  Buck. Return, good Catesby, to the gracious duke: 64
Tell him, myself, the mayor and aldermen,
In deep designs, in matter of great moment,
No less importing than our general good,
Are come to have some conference with his Grace.   68
  Cate. I'll signify so much unto him straight.   *Exit.*
  Buck. Ah, ha, my lord, this prince is not an Edward!
He is not lolling on a lewd love-bed,
But on his knees at meditation;   72
Not dallying with a brace of courtesans,
But meditating with two deep divines;
Not sleeping, to engross his idle body,
But praying, to enrich his watchful soul.   76
Happy were England, would this virtuous prince
Take on his Grace the sovereignty thereof:
But sure, I fear, we shall not win him to it.
  May. Marry, God defend his Grace should say us
    nay!   80
  Buck. I fear he will. Here Catesby comes again.

---

55 dance attendance: *attend assiduously*   69 straight: *at once*
75 engross: *fatten*   79 win: *persuade*

[Re-]enter Catesby.

Now, Catesby, what says his Grace?

Cate. He wonders to what end you have assembled
Such troops of citizens to come to him,   84
His Grace not being warn'd thereof before:
He fears, my lord, you mean no good to him.

Buck. Sorry I am my noble cousin should
Suspect me that I mean no good to him.   88
By heaven, we come to him in perfect love;
And so once more return, and tell his Grace.

Exit [Catesby].

When holy and devout religious men
Are at their beads, 'tis much to draw them thence; 92
So sweet is zealous contemplation.

Enter Richard, aloft, between two Bishops.
[Catesby returns.]

    L. May. See, where his Grace stands 'tween two
       clergymen!

Buck. Two props of virtue for a Christian prince,
To stay him from the fall of vanity;   96
And, see, a book of prayer in his hand:
True ornaments to know a holy man.
Famous Plantagenet, most gracious prince,
Lend favourable ear to our requests,   100
And pardon us the interruption
Of thy devotion and right Christian zeal.

    Rich. My lord, there needs no such apology;
I do beseech your Grace to pardon me,   104
Who, earnest in the service of my God,
Deferr'd the visitation of my friends.
But, leaving this, what is your Grace's pleasure?

92 beads: *prayers*
98 ornaments: *the word refers to the bishops as well as to the
prayer-book*

Buck. Even that, I hope, which pleaseth God
    above,   108
And all good men of this ungovern'd isle.
    Rich. I do suspect I have done some offence
That seems disgracious in the city's eye;
And that you come to reprehend my ignorance.   112
    Buck. You have, my lord: would it might please
    your Grace,
On our entreaties to amend your fault!
    Rich. Else wherefore breathe I in a Christian land?
    Buck. Know then, it is your fault that you resign 116
The supreme seat, the throne majestical,
The sceptred office of your ancestors,
Your state of fortune and your due of birth,
The lineal glory of your royal house,   120
To the corruption of a blemish'd stock;
Whiles, in the mildness of your sleepy thoughts,—
Which here we waken to our country's good,—
The noble isle doth want his proper limbs;   124
His face defac'd with scars of infamy,
His royal stock graft with ignoble plants,
And almost shoulder'd in the swallowing gulf
Of dark forgetfulness and deep oblivion.   128
Which to recure we heartily solicit
Your gracious self to take on you the charge
And kingly government of this your land:
Not as protector, steward, substitute,   132
Or lowly factor for another's gain;
But as successively from blood to blood,
Your right of birth, your empery, your own.
For this, consorted with the citizens,   136

111 disgracious: *ungracious*   124 want: *lack*   his: *its*
126 graft: *engrafted*   128 deep: *profound*
129 recure: *restore (to normal)*   130 charge: *responsibility*
133 factor: *hireling*   134 successively: *by right of succession*
135 empery: *empire*

Your very worshipful and loving friends,
And by their vehement instigation,
In this just cause come I to move your Grace.
   Rich. I cannot tell, if to depart in silence,   140
Or bitterly to speak in your reproof,
Best fitteth my degree or your condition:
If not to answer, you might haply think
Tongue-tied ambition, not replying, yielded   144
To bear the golden yoke of sovereignty,
Which fondly you would here impose on me;
If to reprove you for this suit of yours,
So season'd with your faithful love to me,   148
Then, on the other side, I check'd my friends.
Therefore, to speak, and to avoid the first,
And then, in speaking, not to incur the last,
Definitively thus I answer you.   152
Your love deserves my thanks; but my desert
Unmeritable shuns your high request.
First, if all obstacles were cut away,
And that my path were even to the crown,   156
As the ripe revenue and due of birth,
Yet so much is my poverty of spirit,
So mighty and so many my defects,
That I would rather hide me from my greatness,   160
Being a bark to brook no mighty sea,
Than in my greatness covet to be hid,
And in the vapour of my glory smother'd.
But, God be thank'd, there is no need of me;   164
And much I need to help you, were there need;
The royal tree hath left us royal fruit,
Which, mellow'd by the stealing hours of time,
Will well become the seat of majesty,   168

140-172 *Cf. n.*   142 condition: *rank*
143 haply: *perhaps*   148 season'd with: *rendered palatable by*
149 check'd: *should rebuke*   154 Unmeritable: *undeserving*
157 ripe revenue: *ready inheritance*   165 And . . . need; *cf. n.*

And make, no doubt, us happy by his reign.
On him I lay that you would lay on me,
The right and fortune of his happy stars;
Which God defend that I should wring from him! 172
   Buck. My lord, this argues conscience in your
      Grace;
But the respects thereof are nice and trivial,
All circumstances well considered.
You say that Edward is your brother's son: 176
So say we too, but not by Edward's wife;
For first was he contract to Lady Lucy,—
Your mother lives a witness to his vow,—
And afterward by substitute betroth'd   180
To Bona, sister to the King of France.
These both put off, a poor petitioner,
A care-craz'd mother to a many sons,
A beauty-waning and distressed widow,   184
Even in the afternoon of her best days,
Made prize and purchase of his wanton eye,
Seduc'd the pitch and height of his degree
To base declension and loath'd bigamy: 188
By her, in his unlawful bed, he got
This Edward, whom our manners call the prince.
More bitterly could I expostulate,
Save that, for reverence to some alive,   192
I give a sparing limit to my tongue.
Then, good my lord, take to your royal self
This proffer'd benefit of dignity;
If not to bless us and the land withal,   196
Yet to draw forth your noble ancestry

171 happy stars; *cf. n.*
174 respects . . . nice: *considerations on which your arguments are
      founded are overscrupulous*
178 contract: *contracted; cf. n. line 5*   179 a witness; *cf. n.*
183 care-craz'd: *shattered by care*
186 purchase: *booty*   187 pitch; *cf. n.*
188 declension: *gradual falling away from a high standard*   bigamy;
      cf. n.   191 expostulate: *expound*

From the corruption of abusing times,
Unto a lineal true-derived course.
 L. May. Do, good my lord; your citizens entreat
  you.   200
 Buck. Refuse not, mighty lord, this proffer'd love.
 Cate. O, make them joyful! grant their lawful suit!
 Rich. Alas! why would you heap this care on me?
I am unfit for state and majesty: 204
I do beseech you, take it not amiss,
I cannot nor I will not yield to you.
 Buck. If you refuse it, as, in love and zeal,
Loath to depose the child, your brother's son; 208
As well we know your tenderness of heart
And gentle, kind, effeminate remorse,
Which we have noted in you to your kindred,
And egally, indeed, to all estates,   212
Yet know whe'r you accept our suit or no,
Your brother's son shall never reign our king;
But we will plant some other in the throne,
To the disgrace and downfall of your house: 216
And in this resolution here we leave you.
Come, citizens, we will entreat no more.
      Exeunt [Buckingham and Citizens].
 Cate. Call him again, sweet prince; accept their suit:
If you deny them, all the land will rue it. 220
 Rich. Will you enforce me to a world of cares?
Call them again: I am not made of stones,
But penetrable to your kind entreaties,
Albeit against my conscience and my soul. 224

   [Re-]enter Buckingham and the rest.

Cousin of Buckingham, and sage, grave men,

198 abusing times: *i.e. the period following Edward's marriage to
 Elizabeth*   210 effeminate remorse: *woman-like pity*
212 egally: *equally*   estates: *classes of persons*
217 in this resolution: *with this resolve*

Since you will buckle fortune on my back,
To bear her burthen, whe'r I will or no,
I must have patience to endure the load: 228
But if black scandal or foul-fac'd reproach
Attend the sequel of your imposition,
Your mere enforcement shall acquittance me
From all the impure blots and stains thereof;   232
For God doth know, and you may partly see,
How far I am from the desire of this.

    L. May. God bless your Grace! we see it, and will
      say it.

    Rich. In saying so, you shall but say the truth.   236

    Buck. Then I salute you with this royal title:
Long live King Richard, England's worthy king!

    All. Amen.

    Buck. To-morrow may it please you to be
      crown'd?   240

    Rich. Even when you please, for you will have it so.

    Buck. To-morrow then we will attend your Grace:
And so most joyfully we take our leave.

    Rich. [*To the Bishops.*] Come, let us to our holy
      work again.   244
Farewell, my cousin;—farewell, gentle friends.

                             Exeunt.

230 imposition: *action in imposing this burden*
231 acquittance: *acquit*

ACT FOURTH

Scene One

[London.   Before the Tower]

Enter the Queen [Elizabeth], Anne, Duchess of Gloucester, [leading Lady Margaret Plantagenet], The Duchess of York, and Marquess Dorset.

Duch. York. Who meets us here? my niece Plan-
    tagenet,
Led in the hand of her kind aunt of Gloucester?
Now, for my life, she's wand'ring to the Tower,
On pure heart's love, to greet the tender prince.   4
Daughter, well met.
    Anne.   God give your Graces both
A happy and a joyful time of day!
    Q. Eliz. As much to you, good sister! whither away?
    Anne. No farther than the Tower; and, as I guess,   8
Upon the like devotion as yourselves,
To gratulate the gentle princes there.
    Q. Eliz. Kind sister, thanks: we'll enter all to-
    gether:—

Enter the Lieutenant [Brakenbury].

And, in good time, here the lieutenant comes.   12
Master lieutenant, pray you, by your leave,
How doth the prince, and my young son of York?
    Brak. Right well, dear madam. By your patience,
I may not suffer you to visit them: 16
The king hath strictly charg'd the contrary.
    Q. Eliz. The king! who's that?
    Brak.   I mean the Lord Protector.

1 niece: *grandchild*
9 like devotion; *cf. n.*

4 On: *out of*
10 gratulate: *greet*

Q. Eliz. The Lord protect him from that kingly
    title!
Hath he set bounds between their love and me?   20
I am their mother; who shall bar me from them?
    Duch. York. I am their father's mother; I will see
    them.
    Anne. Their aunt I am in law, in love their mother:
Then bring me to their sights; I'll bear thy blame,   24
And take thy office from thee, on my peril.
    Brak. No, madam, no, I may not leave it so:
I am bound by oath, and therefore pardon me.

                        Exit Lieutenant.

Enter Stanley.

    Stan. Let me but meet you, ladies, one hour hence,   28
And I'll salute your Grace of York as mother,
And reverend looker-on of two fair queens.
[*To the Duchess of Gloucester.*] Come, madam, you
    must straight to Westminster,
There to be crowned Richard's royal queen.   32
    Q. Eliz. Ah! cut my lace asunder,
That my pent heart may have some scope to beat,
Or else I swoon with this dead-killing news.
    Anne. Despiteful tidings! O! unpleasing news!   36
    Dor. Be of good cheer: mother, how fares your
    Grace?
    Q. Eliz. O, Dorset! speak not to me, get thee gone!
Death and destruction dog thee at thy heels;
Thy mother's name is ominous to children.   40
If thou wilt outstrip death, go cross the seas,
And live with Richmond, from the reach of hell:
Go, hie thee, hie thee, from this slaughter-house,
Lest thou increase the number of the dead,   44

26 it: *i.e. my office*   32 crowned; *cf. n.*
35 dead-killing: *death-dealing*   36 Despiteful: *cruel*
42 Richmond; *cf. n.*   from: *beyond*

And make me die the thrall of Margaret's curse,
Nor mother, wife, nor England's counted queen.
   Stan. Full of wise care is this your counsel, madam.
[*To Dorset.*] Take all the swift advantage of the
    hours;   48
You shall have letters from me to my son
In your behalf, to meet you on the way:
Be not ta'en tardy by unwise delay.
   Duch. York. O ill-dispersing wind of misery! 52
O my accursed womb, the bed of death!
A cockatrice hast thou hatch'd to the world,
Whose unavoided eye is murtherous!
   Stan. Come, madam, come; I in all haste was sent. 56
   Anne. And I with all unwillingness will go.
O would to God that the inclusive verge
Of golden metal that must round my brow
Were red-hot steel to sear me to the brains!   60
Anointed let me be with deadly venom,
And die, ere men can say, 'God save the queen!'
   Q. Eliz. Go, go, poor soul, I envy not thy glory;
To feed my humour, wish thyself no harm.   64
   Anne. No! why? When he, that is my husband now
Came to me, as I follow'd Henry's corse;
When scarce the blood was well wash'd from his hands,
Which issu'd from my other angel husband,   68
And that dead saint which then I weeping follow'd;
O! when, I say, I look'd on Richard's face,
This was my wish, 'Be thou,' quoth I, 'accurs'd,
For making me, so young, so old a widow!   72
And, when thou wedd'st, let sorrow haunt thy bed;
And be thy wife—if any be so mad—
More miserable by the life of thee

45 thrall: *slave, victim*   46 counted: *accounted*
54 cockatrice; *cf. n.*   58 verge: *circle*
72 old: *i.e. old in sorrow*   74 *Cf. I. ii. 26-28*

Than thou hast made me by my dear lord's death!'   76
Lo! ere I can repeat this curse again,
Within so small a time, my woman's heart
Grossly grew captive to his honey words,
And prov'd the subject of mine own soul's curse: 80
Which hitherto hath held mine eyes from rest;
For never yet one hour in his bed
Did I enjoy the golden dew of sleep,
But with his timorous dreams was still awak'd.   84
Besides, he hates me for my father Warwick,
And will, no doubt, shortly be rid of me.

 Q. Eliz. Poor heart, adieu! I pity thy complaining.
 Anne. No more than with my soul I mourn for
  yours.   88
 Dor. Farewell! thou woeful welcomer of glory!
 Anne. Adieu, poor soul, that tak'st thy leave of it!
 Duch. York. [*To Dorset.*] Go thou to Richmond,
  and good fortune guide thee!
[*To Anne.*] Go thou to Richard, and good angels tend
 thee!   92
[*To Q. Elizabeth.*] Go thou to sanctuary, and good
 thoughts possess thee!
I to my grave, where peace and rest lie with me!
Eighty odd years of sorrow have I seen,
And each hour's joy wrack'd with a week of teen.   96
 Q. Eliz. Stay, yet look back with me unto the Tower.
Pity, you ancient stones, those tender babes
Whom envy hath immur'd within your walls,
Rough cradle for such little pretty ones!   100
Rude ragged nurse, old sullen playfellow
For tender princes, use my babies well.
So foolish sorrow bids your stones farewell.

           Exeunt.

85 Warwick; *cf. n.*   95 Eighty odd; *cf. n.*
96 wrack'd with: *destroyed by* teen: *woe*
99 envy: *spite*   101 ragged: *rough*   sullen: *dismal*

Scene Two

[*The Same. A Room of State in the Palace*]

Sound a Sennet. Enter Richard in pomp, Buck-
ingham, Catesby, Ratcliff, Lovel [and a Page].

K. Rich. Stand all apart! Cousin of Buckingham!
Buck. My gracious sovereign!
K. Rich. Give me thy hand. *Sound. [He ascends*
  the throne.] Thus high, by thy advice,
And thy assistance, is King Richard seated: 4
But shall we wear these glories for a day?
Or shall they last, and we rejoice in them?
Buck. Still live they, and for ever let them last!
K. Rich. Ah! Buckingham, now do I play the
  touch,   8
To try if thou be current gold indeed:
Young Edward lives: think now what I would speak.
Buck. Say on, my loving lord.
K. Rich. Why, Buckingham, I say, I would be
  king.   12
Buck. Why, so you are, my thrice-renowned lord.
K. Rich. Ha! am I king? 'Tis so: but Edward lives.
Buck. True, noble prince.
K. Rich.   O bitter consequence,
That Edward still should live! 'True, noble prince!' 16
Cousin, thou wast not wont to be so dull:
Shall I be plain? I wish the bastards dead;
And I would have it suddenly perform'd.
What sayst thou now? speak suddenly, be brief.   20
Buck. Your Grace may do your pleasure.
K. Rich. Tut, tut! thou art all ice, thy kindness
  freezes:

8 play the touch: *play the part of a touchstone; cf. n.*
15 consequence: *sequel*

Say, have I thy consent that they shall die?

   Buck. Give me some little breath, some pause, dear
    lord,   24

Before I positively speak in this:

I will resolve you herein presently.   *Exit Buck.*

   Cate. [*Aside to another.*] The king is angry: see, he
    gnaws his lip.

   K. Rich. [*Descends from his throne.*] I will con-
    verse with iron-witted fools   28

And unrespective boys: none are for me

That look into me with considerate eyes.

High-reaching Buckingham grows circumspect.

Boy!   32

   Page. My lord!

   K. Rich. Know'st thou not any whom corrupting
    gold

Will tempt unto a close exploit of death?

   Page. I know a discontented gentleman,   36

Whose humble means match not his haughty spirit:

Gold were as good as twenty orators,

And will, no doubt, tempt him to anything.

   K. Rich. What is his name?

   Page.   His name, my lord, is Tyrrell. 40

   K. Rich. I partly know the man: go, call him hither,
    boy.   *Exit* [*Page*].

The deep-revolving, witty Buckingham

No more shall be the neighbour to my counsels.

Hath he so long held out with me, untir'd,   44

And stops he now for breath? well, be it so.

Enter Stanley.

How now, Lord Stanley! what's the news?

---

26 resolve you: *give you a definite answer*
29 unrespective: *heedless*   31 High-reaching: *ambitious*
35 close: *secret*   exploit: *deed*   40 *Cf. n.*
42 deep-revolving: *profoundly considering*   witty: *cunning*

Stan. Know, my loving lord,
The Marquess Dorset, as I hear, is fled   48
To Richmond, in the parts where he abides.
  K. Rich. Come hither, Catesby: rumour it abroad
That Anne, my wife, is very grievous sick;
I will take order for her keeping close.   52
Inquire me out some mean poor gentleman,
Whom I will marry straight to Clarence' daughter:
The boy is foolish, and I fear not him.
Look, how thou dream'st! I say again, give out   56
That Anne, my queen, is sick, and like to die.
About it; for it stands me much upon
To stop all hopes whose growth may damage me.
                                          [*Exit Catesby.*]
I must be married to my brother's daughter,   60
Or else my kingdom stands on brittle glass.
Murther her brothers, and then marry her!
Uncertain way of gain! But I am in
So far in blood, that sin will pluck on sin: 64
Tear-falling pity dwells not in this eye.

                [Re-]enter [Page with] Tyrrell.

Is thy name Tyrrell?
  Tyr. James Tyrrell, and your most obedient subject.
  K. Rich. Art thou, indeed?
  Tyr.   Prove me, my gracious lord. 68
  K. Rich. Dar'st thou resolve to kill a friend of mine?
  Tyr. Please you; but I had rather kill two enemies.
  K. Rich. Why, then thou hast it: two deep enemies,
Foes to my rest, and my sweet sleep's disturbers,   72
Are they that I would have thee deal upon.
Tyrrell, I mean those bastards in the Tower.
  Tyr. Let me have open means to come to them,

51 grievous sick; *cf. n.*   58 stands . . . upon: *concerns me greatly*
60 brother's daughter; *cf. n.*   65 Tear-falling: *causing tears to fall*
68 Prove: *test*   73 deal upon: *set to work on*

And soon I'll rid you from the fear of them.   76

    K. Rich. Thou sing'st sweet music. Hark, come
      hither, Tyrrell:

Go, by this token: rise, and lend thine ear.   *Whispers.*

There is no more but so: say it is done,

And I will love thee, and prefer thee for it.   80

    Tyr. I will dispatch it straight.   *Exit.*

           [Re-]enter Buckingham.

    Buck. My lord, I have consider'd in my mind

The late request that you did sound me in.

    K. Rich. Well, let that rest. Dorset is fled to Rich-
      mond.   84

    Buck. I hear the news, my lord.

    K. Rich. Stanley, he is your wife's son: well, look
      to it.

    Buck. My lord, I claim the gift, my due by promise,

For which your honour and your faith is pawn'd: 88

Th' earldom of Hereford and the moveables

Which you have promised I shall possess.

    K. Rich. Stanley, look to your wife: if she convey

Letters to Richmond, you shall answer it.   92

    Buck. What says your highness to my just request?

    K. Rich. I do remember me, Henry the Sixth

Did prophesy that Richmond should be king,

When Richmond was a little peevish boy.   96

A king! perhaps—

    [*Buck.* My lord!

    K. Rich. How chance the prophet could not at that
      time

Have told me, I being by, that I should kill him?   100

---

79 There . . . so: *i.e. nothing more than to carry out the whispered
    instructions*   80 prefer: *advance*
88 pawn'd: *pledged*   91 wife; *cf. n.*
92 answer: *answer for*   94 remember me: *recollect*
95 prophesy; *cf. n.*   98-115 *Cf. n.*
99 How chance: *how chances it that*

Buck. My lord, your promise for the earldom,—

K. Rich. Richmond! When last I was at Exeter,
The mayor in courtesy show'd me the castle,
And call'd it Rougemont: at which name I started, 104
Because a bard of Ireland told me once
I should not live long after I saw Richmond.

Buck. My lord!

K. Rich. Ay, what's o'clock? 108

Buck. I am thus bold to put your Grace in mind
Of what you promis'd me.

K. Rich. Well, but what is 't o'clock?

Buck.   Upon the stroke of ten.

K. Rich. Well, let it strike.

Buck.   Why let it strike? 112

K. Rich. Because that, like a Jack, thou keep'st the
    stroke
Betwixt thy begging and my meditation.
I am not in the giving vein to-day.]

Buck. May it please you to resolve me in my
    suit? 116

K. Rich. Thou troublest me: I am not in the vein.

                     Exit [*King Richard and Train*].

Buck. And is it thus? repays he my deep service
With such contempt? made I him king for this?
O, let me think on Hastings, and be gone 120
To Brecknock, while my fearful head is on.   *Exit.*

104 Rougemont; *cf. n.*   113 Jack; *cf. n.*
116 resolve: *confirm; cf. n.*   121 Brecknock; *cf. n.*

Scene Three

[*The Same.*]

Enter Tyrrell.

Tyr. The tyrannous and bloody act is done;
The most arch deed of piteous massacre
That ever yet this land was guilty of.
Dighton and Forrest, whom I did suborn   4
To do this piece of ruthful butchery,
Albeit they were flesh'd villains, bloody dogs,
Melted with tenderness and mild compassion,
Wept like to children in their death's sad story.   8
'Oh! thus,' quoth Dighton, 'lay the gentle babes:'
'Thus, thus,' quoth Forrest, 'girdling one another
Within their alabaster innocent arms:
Their lips were four red roses on a stalk,   12
And in their summer beauty kiss'd each other.
A book of prayers on their pillow lay;
Which one,' quoth Forrest, 'almost chang'd my mind;
But, O, the devil'——there the villain stopp'd;   16
When Dighton thus told on: 'We smothered
The most replenished sweet work of nature,
That from the prime creation e'er she fram'd.'
Hence both are gone with conscience and remorse; 20
They could not speak; and so I left them both,
To bear this tidings to the bloody king:
And here he comes.

Enter Richard.

All health, my sovereign lord!

2 arch: *principal*   4 suborn: *procure by bribery*
5 ruthful: *pitiable*   6 flesh'd: *hardened; cf. n.*
8 in: *in relating*   9 Dighton; *cf. n.*   10 Forrest; *cf. n.*
11 alabaster: *marble-white*   18 replenished: *complete, perfect*
19 prime: *first in time*   fram'd: *formed*
20 gone: *completely overcome*

K. Rich. Kind Tyrrell, am I happy in thy news? 24

Tyr. If to have done the thing you gave in charge
Beget your happiness, be happy, then,
For it is done.

K. Rich.   But didst thou see them dead?

Tyr. I did, my lord.

K. Rich.   And buried, gentle Tyrrell? 28

Tyr. The chaplain of the Tower hath buried them;
But where, to say the truth, I do not know.

K. Rich. Come to me, Tyrrell, soon, and after sup-
          per,
When thou shalt tell the process of their death.   32
Meantime, but think how I may do thee good,
And be inheritor of thy desire.
Farewell till then.

Tyr.   I humbly take my leave. [*Exit.*]

K. Rich. The son of Clarence have I pent up
          close;   36
His daughter meanly have I match'd in marriage;
The sons of Edward sleep in Abraham's bosom;
And Anne, my wife, hath bid this world good night.
Now, for I know the Britaine Richmond aims   40
At young Elizabeth, my brother's daughter,
And, by that knot, looks proudly on the crown,
To her go I, a jolly thriving wooer.

Enter Ratcliff.

Rat. My lord!   44

K. Rich. Good or bad news, that thou com'st in so
          bluntly?

Rat. Bad news, my lord: Morton is fled to Rich-
          mond;

32 process: *narrative*   34 inheritor: *possessor*
36 pent up; *cf. n.*   37 daughter; *cf. n.*
38 Abraham's bosom; *cf. n.*   40 Britaine: *Breton; cf. n.*
42 knot: *i.e. marriage alliance*   43 S. d. Ratcliff; *cf. n.*
46 Morton: *John Morton, Bishop of Ely; cf. n.*

And Buckingham, back'd with the hardy Welshmen,
Is in the field, and still his power increaseth.   48

   K. Rich. Ely with Richmond troubles me more near
Than Buckingham and his rash-levied strength.
Come; I have learn'd that fearful commenting
Is leaden servitor to dull delay.   52
Delay leads impotent and snail-pac'd beggary:
Then fiery expedition be my wing,
Jove's Mercury, and herald for a king!
Go, muster men: my counsel is my shield;   56
We must be brief when traitors brave the field.

                                      Exeunt.

Scene Four

[The Same. Before the Palace]

Enter old Queen Margaret.

   Q. Mar. So, now prosperity begins to mellow
And drop into the rotten mouth of death.
Here in these confines slily have I lurk'd
To watch the waning of mine enemies.   4
A dire induction am I witness to,
And will to France, hoping the consequence
Will prove as bitter, black, and tragical.
Withdraw thee, wretched Margaret: who comes
    here?   8

Enter Duchess [of York] and Queen [Elizabeth].

   Q. Eliz. Ah! my poor princes! ah, my tender babes,
My unblown flowers, new-appearing sweets,

---

48 power: *body of troops; cf. n.*   49 near: *closely*
50 rash-levied: *hastily raised*
51 fearful commenting: *timorous discussion*
52 leaden: *figuratively for 'slow'*   54 expedition: *haste*
55 Jove's Mercury; *cf. n.*   57 brave: *boastfully dispute*
3 confines: *regions, territories*   6 to France; *cf. n.*
10 unblown: *unblossomed, budding*

If yet your gentle souls fly in the air
And be not fix'd in doom perpetual,   12
Hover about me with your airy wings,
And hear your mother's lamentation.

   Q. Mar. Hover about her; say, that right for right
Hath dimm'd your infant morn to aged night.   16

   Duch. So many miseries have craz'd my voice,
That my woe-wearied tongue is still and mute.
Edward Plantagenet, why art thou dead?

   Q. Mar. Plantagenet doth quit Plantagenet;   20
Edward for Edward pays a dying debt.

   Q. Eliz. Wilt thou, O God! fly from such gentle
     lambs,
And throw them in the entrails of the wolf?
When didst thou sleep when such a deed was done? 24

   Q. Mar. When holy Harry died, and my sweet son.

   Duch. Dead life, blind sight, poor mortal living
     ghost,
Woe's scene, world's shame, grave's due by life
     usurp'd,
Brief abstract and record of tedious days,   28
Rest thy unrest on England's lawful earth,
                [Sitting down.]
Unlawfully made drunk with innocent blood!

   Q. Eliz. Ah! that thou wouldst as soon afford a
     grave
As thou canst yield a melancholy seat;   32
Then would I hide my bones, not rest them here.
Ah! who hath any cause to mourn but we?
              [Sitting down by her.]

   Q. Mar. If ancient sorrow be most reverend,
Give mine the benefit of signiory,   36

15 right for right; *cf. n.*   17 craz'd: *cracked*
20 quit: *requite*   28 abstract: *epitome; cf. n.*
31 thou: *i.e. the earth*   36 signiory: *precedence*

And let my griefs frown on the upper hand,
If sorrow can admit society.

> [*Sitting down with them.*]

[Tell o'er your woes again by viewing mine:]
I had an Edward, till a Richard kill'd him;   40
I had a husband, till a Richard kill'd him:
Thou hadst an Edward, till a Richard kill'd him;
Thou hadst a Richard, till a Richard kill'd him.

> *Duch.* I had a Richard too, and thou didst kill
> him;   44

I had a Rutland too, thou holp'st to kill him.

> *Q. Mar.* Thou hadst a Clarence too, and Richard
> kill'd him.

From forth the kennel of thy womb hath crept
A hell-hound that doth hunt us all to death: 48
That dog, that had his teeth before his eyes,
To worry lambs, and lap their gentle blood,
That foul defacer of God's handiwork,
That reigns in galled eyes of weeping souls,   52
That excellent grand-tyrant of the earth,
Thy womb let loose, to chase us to our graves.
O upright, just, and true-disposing God!
How do I thank thee that this carnal cur   56
Preys on the issue of his mother's body,
And makes her pew-fellow with others' moan.

> *Duch.* O, Harry's wife, triumph not in my woes!

God witness with me, I have wept for thine.   60

> *Q. Mar.* Bear with me; I am hungry for revenge,
> And now I cloy me with beholding it.

Thy Edward he is dead, that kill'd my Edward;
The other Edward dead, to quit my Edward;   64

37 on . . . hand: *in the first place*   52, 53 *Cf. n.*
52 galled: *sore from weeping; cf. n.*   53 excellent: *superlative*
56 carnal: *bloody*   58 pew-fellow: *associate*
64 The: *misprint for 'thy' (?)*

Young York he is but boot, because both they
Match'd not the high perfection of my loss:
Thy Clarence he is dead that stabb'd my Edward;
And the beholders of this frantic play,   68
Th' adulterate Hastings, Rivers, Vaughan, Grey,
Untimely smother'd in their dusky graves.
Richard yet lives, hell's black intelligencer,
Only reserv'd their factor, to buy souls   72
And send them thither; but at hand, at hand,
Ensues his piteous and unpitied end:
Earth gapes, hell burns, fiends roar, saints pray,
To have him suddenly convey'd from hence.   76
Cancel his bond of life, dear God! I pray,
That I may live and say, The dog is dead.

    Q. Eliz. O! thou didst prophesy the time would
       come
That I should wish for thee to help me curse   80
That bottled spider, that foul bunchback'd toad.

    Q. Mar. I call'd thee then vain flourish of my for-
       tune;
I call'd thee then poor shadow, painted queen;
The presentation of but what I was;   84
The flattering index of a direful pageant;
One heav'd a-high to be hurl'd down below;
A mother only mock'd with two fair babes;
A dream of what thou wast, a garish flag   88
To be the aim of every dangerous shot;
A sign of dignity, a breath, a bubble,
A queen in jest, only to fill the scene.
Where is thy husband now? where be thy brothers? 92
Where be thy two sons? wherein dost thou joy?
Who sues and kneels and says, 'God save the queen'?

---

65 boot: *something given in addition, to make up a deficiency of value*
69 adulterate: *adulterous*   71 intelligencer: *secret agent, spy*
72 their: *refers to hell*   84 presentation: *semblance*
85 index . . . pageant; *cf. n.*   88-90 *Cf. n.*   88 garish: *gaudy*

Where be the bending peers that flatter'd thee?
Where be the thronging troops that follow'd thee? 96
Decline all this, and see what now thou art:
For happy wife, a most distressed widow;
For joyful mother, one that wails the name;
For one being sued to, one that humbly sues; 100
For queen, a very caitiff crown'd with care;
For she that scorn'd at me, now scorn'd of me;
For she being fear'd of all, now fearing one;
For she commanding all, obey'd of none. 104
Thus hath the course of justice whirl'd about,
And left thee but a very prey to time;
Having no more but thought of what thou wast,
To torture thee the more, being what thou art. 108
Thou didst usurp my place, and dost thou not
Usurp the just proportion of my sorrow?
Now thy proud neck bears half my burthen'd yoke,
From which even here I slip my wearied head, 112
And leave the burthen of it all on thee.
Farewell, York's wife, and queen of sad mischance:
These English woes shall make me smile in France.

    Q. Eliz. O thou, well skill'd in curses, stay awhile, 116
And teach me how to curse mine enemies.

    Q. Mar. Forbear to sleep the night, and fast the day;
Compare dead happiness with living woe;
Think that thy babes were sweeter than they were, 120
And he that slew them fouler than he is:
Bettering thy loss makes the bad causer worse:
Revolving this will teach thee how to curse.

    Q. Eliz. My words are dull; O! quicken them with thine! 124

97 Decline: *go through formally*
101 caitiff: *wretch (literally, captive)*
105 *Cf. n.*
118 the: *during the*
122 Bettering: *magnifying*
123 Revolving: *thinking over*
124 quicken: *enliven*

Q. Mar. Thy woes will make them sharp, and pierce
   like mine.   *Exit Margaret.*
Duch. Why should calamity be full of words?
Q. Eliz. Windy attorneys to their clients' woes,
Airy succeeders of intestate joys,   128
Poor breathing orators of miseries!
Let them have scope: though what they will impart
Help nothing else, yet do they ease the heart.
Duch. If so, then be not tongue-tied: go with me, 132
And in the breath of bitter words let's smother
My damned son, that thy two sweet sons smother'd.
                          [*A trumpet heard.*]
The trumpet sounds: be copious in exclaims.

Enter King Richard and his Train [marching].

K. Rich. Who intercepts me in my expedition? 136
Duch. O! she that might have intercepted thee,
By strangling thee in her accursed womb,
From all the slaughters, wretch, that thou hast done!
Q. Eliz. Hid'st thou that forehead with a golden
   crown,   140
Where should be branded, if that right were right,
The slaughter of the prince that ow'd that crown,
And the dire death of my poor sons and brothers?
Tell me, thou villain slave, where are my children? 144
Duch. Thou toad, thou toad, where is thy brother
   Clarence
And little Ned Plantagenet, his son?
Q. Eliz. Where is the gentle Rivers, Vaughan, Grey?
Duch. Where is kind Hastings?   148
K. Rich. A flourish, trumpets! strike alarum, drums!
Let not the heavens hear these tell-tale women

128 intestate: *literally, not having made a will; cf. n.*
131 Help . . . else: *is of no avail otherwise*
142 ow'd: *owned*   148 *Cf. n*

Rail on the Lord's anointed. Strike, I say!

Flourish. Alarums.

Either be patient, and entreat me fair,   152
Or with the clamorous report of war
Thus will I drown your exclamations.

   Duch. Art thou my son?

   K. Rich. Ay; I thank God, my father, and your-
    self.   156

   Duch. Then patiently hear my impatience.

   K. Rich. Madam, I have a touch of your condition,
That cannot brook the accent of reproof.

   Duch. O, let me speak!

   K. Rich.   Do, then; but I'll not hear. 160

   Duch. I will be mild and gentle in my words.

   K. Rich. And brief, good mother; for I am in haste.

   Duch. Art thou so hasty? I have stay'd for thee,
God knows, in torment and in agony.   164

   K. Rich. And came I not at last to comfort you?

   Duch. No, by the holy rood, thou know'st it well,
Thou cam'st on earth to make the earth my hell.
A grievous burthen was thy birth to me;   168
Tetchy and wayward was thy infancy;
Thy school-days frightful, desperate, wild and fu-
   rious;
Thy prime of manhood daring, bold, and venturous;
Thy age confirm'd, proud, subtle, sly, and bloody, 172
More mild, but yet more harmful, kind in hatred.
What comfortable hour canst thou name
That ever grac'd me with thy company?

   K. Rich. Faith, none, but Humphrey Hour, that
    call'd your Grace   176

---

152 entreat me fair: *use me well*   158 condition: *temperament*
163 stay'd: *waited*   169 Tetchy: *fretful, peevish*
171 prime of: *early*
173 kind in hatred: *i.e. hating while pretending kindness*
176 Humphrey Hour; *cf. n.*

To breakfast once forth of my company.
If I be so disgracious in your eye,
Let me march on, and not offend you, madam.
Strike up the drum!
 Duch.   I prithee, hear me speak. 180
 K. Rich. You speak too bitterly.
 Duch.   Hear me a word;
For I shall never speak to thee again.
 K. Rich. So!
 Duch. Either thou wilt die by God's just ordi-
  nance, 184
Ere from this war thou turn a conqueror;
Or I with grief and extreme age shall perish,
And never more behold thy face again.
Therefore take with thee my most grievous curse, 188
Which, in the day of battle, tire thee more
Than all the complete armour that thou wear'st!
My prayers on the adverse party fight;
And there the little souls of Edward's children 192
Whisper the spirits of thine enemies
And promise them success and victory.
Bloody thou art, bloody will be thy end;
Shame serves thy life and doth thy death attend. 196
            Exit.
 Q. Eliz. Though far more cause, yet much less spirit
  to curse
Abides in me: I say amen to her.   [*Going.*]
 K. Rich. Stay, madam; I must talk a word with you.
 Q. Eliz. I have no more sons of the royal blood 200
For thee to slaughter: for my daughters, Richard,
They shall be praying nuns, not weeping queens;
And therefore level not to hit their lives.
 K. Rich. You have a daughter call'd Elizabeth, 204

178 disgracious: *out of favor*   196 serves: *i.e. is servant to*
203 level: *aim*   204 Elizabeth; *cf. n.*

Virtuous and fair, royal and gracious.

    Q. Eliz. And must she die for this? O! let her live,
And I'll corrupt her manners, stain her beauty;
Slander myself as false to Edward's bed;   208
Throw over her the veil of infamy:
So she may live unscarr'd of bleeding slaughter,
I will confess she was not Edward's daughter.

    K. Rich. Wrong not her birth; she is a royal prin-
        cess.   212

    Q. Eliz. To save her life, I'll say she is not so.

    K. Rich. Her life is safest only in her birth.

    Q. Eliz. And only in that safety died her brothers.

    K. Rich. Lo! at their birth good stars were oppo-
        site.   216

    Q. Eliz. No, to their lives ill friends were contrary.

    K. Rich. All unavoided is the doom of destiny.

    Q. Eliz. True, when avoided grace makes destiny.
My babes were destin'd to a fairer death,   220
If grace had bless'd thee with a fairer life.

    K. Rich. You speak as if that I had slain my cousins.

    Q. Eliz. Cousins, indeed; and by their uncle cozen'd
Of comfort, kingdom, kindred, freedom, life.   224
Whose hand soever lanch'd their tender hearts,
Thy head, all indirectly, gave direction:
No doubt the murderous knife was dull and blunt
Till it was whetted on thy stone-hard heart,   228
To revel in the entrails of my lambs.
But that still use of grief makes wild grief tame,
My tongue should to thy ears not name my boys
Till that my nails were anchor'd in thine eyes;   232
And I, in such a desperate bay of death,
Like a poor bark, of sails and tackling reft,

Rush all to pieces on thy rocky bosom.

   K. Rich. Madam, so thrive I in my enterprise 236
And dangerous success of bloody wars,
As I intend more good to you and yours
Than ever you or yours by me were harm'd.

   Q. Eliz. What good is cover'd with the face of
      heaven,   240
To be discover'd, that can do me good?

   K. Rich. Th' advancement of your children, gentle
      lady.

   Q. Eliz. Up to some scaffold, there to lose their
      heads?

   K. Rich. Unto the dignity and height of fortune, 244
The high imperial type of this earth's glory.

   Q. Eliz. Flatter my sorrow with report of it:
Tell me what state, what dignity, what honour,
Canst thou demise to any child of mine?   248

   K. Rich. Even all I have; ay, and myself and all,
Will I withal endow a child of thine;
So in the Lethe of thy angry soul
Thou drown the sad remembrance of those wrongs 252
Which thou supposest I have done to thee.

   Q. Eliz. Be brief, lest that the process of thy kind-
      ness
Last longer telling than thy kindness' date.

   K. Rich. Then know, that from my soul I love thy
      daughter.   256

   Q. Eliz. My daughter's mother thinks it with her
      soul.

   K. Rich. What do you think?

   Q. Eliz. That thou dost love my daughter from thy
      soul:

236-239 *Cf. n.*   237 success: *result*
245 type: *emblem (crown)*   248 demise: *convey*
251 Lethe; *cf. n.*   259 from: *apart from*

So from thy soul's love didst thou love her
   brothers;   260
And from my heart's love I do thank thee for it.

   K. Rich. Be not so hasty to confound my meaning:
I mean, that with my soul I love thy daughter,
And do intend to make her Queen of England.   264

   Q. Eliz. Well then, who dost thou mean shall be
   her king?

   K. Rich. Even he that makes her queen: who else
   should be?

   Q. Eliz. What! thou?

   K. Rich. Even so: how think you of it?   268

   Q. Eliz. How canst thou woo her?

   K. Rich.   That I would learn of you,
As one being best acquainted with her humour.

   Q. Eliz. And wilt thou learn of me?

   K. Rich.   Madam, with all my heart.

   Q. Eliz. Send to her, by the man that slew her
   brothers,   272
A pair of bleeding hearts; thereon engrave
Edward and York; then haply will she weep:
Therefore present to her, as sometime Margaret
Did to thy father, steep'd in Rutland's blood,   276
A handkerchief, which, say to her, did drain
The purple sap from her sweet brother's body,
And bid her wipe her weeping eyes withal.
If this inducement move her not to love,   280
Send her a letter of thy noble deeds:
Tell her thou mad'st away her uncle Clarence,
Her uncle Rivers; ay, and for her sake,
Mad'st quick conveyance with her good aunt Anne.   284

   K. Rich. You mock me, madam; this is not the way
To win your daughter.

   Q. Eliz.   There is no other way,

276 *Cf. n.*   284 conveyance: *i.e. dishonest dealing; cf. n.*

Unless thou couldst put on some other shape,
And not be Richard that hath done all this.   288

   K. Rich. Say, that I did all this for love of her?

   Q. Eliz. Nay, then, indeed, she cannot choose but
    hate thee,

Having bought love with such a bloody spoil.

   K. Rich. Look, what is done cannot be now
    amended: 292

Men shall deal unadvisedly sometimes,
Which after-hours gives leisure to repent.
If I did take the kingdom from your sons,
To make amends I'll give it to your daughter.   296
If I have kill'd the issue of your womb,
To quicken your increase, I will beget
Mine issue of your blood upon your daughter:
A grandam's name is little less in love   300
Than is the doting title of a mother;
They are as children but one step below,
Even of your mettle, of your very blood;
Of all one pain, save for a night of groans   304
Endur'd of her for whom you bid like sorrow.
Your children were vexation to your youth,
But mine shall be a comfort to your age.
The loss you have is but a son being king,   308
And by that loss your daughter is made queen.
I cannot make you what amends I would,
Therefore accept such kindness as I can.
Dorset, your son, that with a fearful soul   312
Leads discontented steps in foreign soil,
This fair alliance quickly shall call home
To high promotions and great dignity:
The king that calls your beauteous daughter wife   316
Familiarly shall call thy Dorset brother;

289 *Cf. n.*   291 spoil: *waste, havoc*
304 Of . . . pain: *of equal interest and responsibility*
305 bid: *offered*   312 Dorset; *cf. n.*

Again shall you be mother to a king,
And all the ruins of distressful times
Repair'd with double riches of content.   320
What! we have many goodly days to see:
The liquid drops of tears that you have shed
Shall come again, transform'd to orient pearl,
Advantaging their love with interest   324
Of ten times double gain of happiness.
Go then, my mother; to thy daughter go:
Make bold her bashful years with your experience;
Prepare her ears to hear a wooer's tale;   328
Put in her tender heart th' aspiring flame
Of golden sovereignty; acquaint the princess
With the sweet silent hours of marriage joys:
And when this arm of mine hath chastised   332
The petty rebel, dull-brain'd Buckingham,
Bound with triumphant garlands will I come,
And lead thy daughter to a conqueror's bed;
To whom I will retail my conquest won,   336
And she shall be sole victress, Cæsar's Cæsar.

   Q. Eliz. What were I best to say? her father's
    brother
Would be her lord? Or shall I say, her uncle?
Or, he that slew her brothers and her uncles?   340
Under what title shall I woo for thee,
That God, the law, my honour, and her love
Can make seem pleasing to her tender years?

   K. Rich. Infer fair England's peace by this alli-
    ance.   344

   Q. Eliz. Which she shall purchase with still lasting
    war.

   K. Rich. Tell her, the king, that may command,
    entreats.

324 love; *cf. n.*   333 *Cf. n.*

Q. Eliz. That at her hands which the king's King forbids.

K. Rich. Say, she shall be a high and mighty queen.   348

Q. Eliz. To vail the title, as her mother doth.

K. Rich. Say, I will love her everlastingly.

Q. Eliz. But how long shall that title 'ever' last?

K. Rich. Sweetly in force unto her fair life's end.   352

Q. Eliz. But how long fairly shall her sweet life last?

K. Rich. As long as heaven and nature lengthens it.

Q. Eliz. As long as hell and Richard likes of it.

K. Rich. Say, I, her sovereign, am her subject low.   356

Q. Eliz. But she, your subject, loathes such sovereignty.

K. Rich. Be eloquent in my behalf to her.

Q. Eliz. An honest tale speeds best being plainly told.

K. Rich. Then plainly to her tell my loving tale. 360

Q. Eliz. Plain and not honest is too harsh a style.

K. Rich. Your reasons are too shallow and too quick.

Q. Eliz. O, no! my reasons are too deep and dead;
Too deep and dead, poor infants, in their graves.   364

K. Rich. Harp not on that string, madam; that is past.

Q. Eliz. Harp on it still shall I till heartstrings break.

K. Rich. Now, by my George, my garter, and my crown,—

Q. Eliz. Profan'd, dishonour'd, and the third usurp'd.   368

347 king's . . . forbids; *cf. n.*
362 quick: *hasty*   365, 366 *Cf. n.*   349 vail: *lower*
                                               367 George; *cf. n.*

K. Rich. I swear,—

Q. Eliz.   By nothing; for this is no oath.
Thy George, profan'd, hath lost his lordly honour;
Thy garter, blemish'd, pawn'd his knightly virtue;
Thy crown, usurp'd, disgrac'd his kingly glory.   372
If something thou wouldst swear to be believ'd,
Swear, then, by something that thou hast not
    wrong'd.

K. Rich. Then, by myself,—

Q. Eliz.   Thyself is self-misus'd.

K. Rich. Now, by the world,—

Q. Eliz.   'Tis full of thy foul wrongs. 376

K. Rich. My father's death,—

Q. Eliz.   Thy life hath it dishonour'd.

K. Rich. Why, then, by God,—

Q. Eliz.   God's wrong is most of all.
If thou didst fear to break an oath with him,
The unity the king my husband made   380
Thou hadst not broken, nor my brothers died:
If thou hadst fear'd to break an oath by him,
Th' imperial metal, circling now thy head,
Had grac'd the tender temples of my child,   384
And both the princes had been breathing here,
Which now, two tender bed-fellows for dust,
Thy broken faith hath made the prey for worms.
What canst thou swear by now?

K. Rich.   The time to come. 388

Q. Eliz. That thou hast wronged in the time o'er-
    past;
For I myself have many tears to wash
Hereafter time for time past wrong'd by thee.
The children live, whose fathers thou hast slaugh-
    ter'd,   392

375 *Cf. n.*   378 God; *cf. n.*
381 brothers; *cf. n.*   391 Hereafter time: *the future*

Ungovern'd youth, to wail it with their age:
The parents live, whose children thou hast butcher'd,
Old barren plants, to wail it with their age.
Swear not by time to come; for that thou hast   396
Misus'd ere us'd, by times ill-us'd o'erpast.
    K. Rich. As I intend to prosper, and repent,
So thrive I in my dangerous affairs
Of hostile arms! myself myself confound!   400
Heaven and fortune bar me happy hours!
Day, yield me not thy light; nor, night, thy rest!
Be opposite all planets of good luck
To my proceeding, if, with dear heart's love,   404
Immaculate devotion, holy thoughts,
I tender not thy beauteous princely daughter!
In her consists my happiness and thine;
Without her, follows to myself, and thee,   408
Herself, the land, and many a Christian soul,
Death, desolation, ruin, and decay:
It cannot be avoided but by this;
It will not be avoided but by this.   412
Therefore, dear mother,—I must call you so,—
Be the attorney of my love to her:
Plead what I will be, not what I have been;
Not my deserts, but what I will deserve: 416
Urge the necessity and state of times,
And be not peevish found in great designs.
    Q. Eliz. Shall I be tempted of the devil thus?
    K. Rich. Ay, if the devil tempt you to do good.   420
    Q. Eliz. Shall I forget myself to be myself?
    K. Rich. Ay, if your self's remembrance wrong
      yourself.
    Q. Eliz. Yet thou didst kill my children.

397 *Cf. n.*   401 *Cf. n.*
406 tender: *hold in high estimation*   418 found; *cf. n.*

K. Rich. But in your daughter's womb I bury
    them: 424
Where, in that nest of spicery, they will breed
Selves of themselves, to your recomforture.

Q. Eliz. Shall I go win my daughter to thy will?

K. Rich. And be a happy mother by the deed.   428

Q. Eliz. I go. Write to me very shortly,
And you shall understand from me her mind.

K. Rich. Bear her my true love's kiss; and so fare-
    well.

                              Exit Q[ueen Elizabeth].

Relenting fool, and shallow changing woman!   432

Enter Ratcliff [followed by Catesby].

How now! what news?

Rat. Most mighty sovereign, on the western coast
Rideth a puissant navy; to our shores
Throng many doubtful hollow-hearted friends,   436
Unarm'd, and unresolv'd to beat them back.
'Tis thought that Richmond is their admiral;
And there they hull, expecting but the aid
Of Buckingham to welcome them ashore.   440

K. Rich. Some light-foot friend post to the Duke of
    Norfolk:
Ratcliff, thyself, or Catesby; where is he?

Cate. Here, my good lord.

K. Rich.   Catesby, fly to the duke.

Cate. I will, my lord, with all convenient haste. 444

K. Rich. Ratcliff, come hither. Post to Salisbury:
When thou com'st thither,—[*To Catesby.*] Dull, un-
    mindful villain,
Why stay'st thou here, and go'st not to the duke?

425 *Cf. n.*   426 recomforture: *renewed comfort*
439 hull: *drift; cf. n.*   441 light-foot: *nimble*   Norfolk; *cf. n.*
445 Ratcliff; *cf. n.*   Salisbury; *cf. n.*

Cate. First, mighty liege, tell me your highness'
    pleasure,   448
What from your Grace I shall deliver to him.

K. Rich. O, true, good Catesby! bid him levy
    straight
The greatest strength and power that he can make,
And meet me suddenly at Salisbury.   452

Cate. I go.   *Exit*.

Rat. What, may it please you, shall I do at Salis-
    bury?

K. Rich. Why, what wouldst thou do there before I
    go?

Rat. Your highness told me I should post before. 456

K. Rich. My mind is chang'd.

> *Enter Lord Stanley.*

                Stanley, what news with you?

Stan. None good, my liege, to please you with the
    hearing;
Nor none so bad but well may be reported.

K. Rich. Hoyday, a riddle! neither good nor bad! 460
What need'st thou run so many miles about,
When thou mayst tell thy tale the nearest way?
Once more, what news?

Stan.   Richmond is on the seas.

K. Rich. There let him sink, and be the seas on
    him!   464
White-liver'd runagate! what doth he there?

Stan. I know not, mighty sovereign, but by guess.

K. Rich. Well, as you guess?

Stan. Stirr'd up by Dorset, Buckingham, and Mor-
    ton,   468
He makes for England, here to claim the crown.

452 suddenly: *immediately*   460 Hoyday: *exclamation of surprise*
465 White-liver'd runagate: *cowardly roamer*

K. Rich. Is the chair empty? is the sword unsway'd?
Is the king dead? the empire unpossess'd?
What heir of York is there alive but we?   472
And who is England's king but great York's heir?
Then, tell me, what makes he upon the seas?

   Stan. Unless for that, my liege, I cannot guess.

   K. Rich. Unless for that he comes to be your
     liege,   476
You cannot guess wherefore the Welshman comes.
Thou wilt revolt and fly to him I fear.

   Stan. No, my good lord; therefore mistrust me not.

   K. Rich. Where is thy power, then, to beat him
     back?   480
Where be thy tenants and thy followers?
Are they not now upon the western shore,
Safe-conducting the rebels from their ships?

   Stan. No, my good lord, my friends are in the
     north.   484

   K. Rich. Cold friends to me: what do they in the
     north,
When they should serve their sovereign in the west?

   Stan. They have not been commanded, mighty king:
Pleaseth your majesty to give me leave,   488
I'll muster up my friends, and meet your Grace,
Where and what time your majesty shall please.

   K. Rich. Ay, [ay,] thou wouldst be gone to join
     with Richmond:
But I'll not trust thee.

   Stan.   Most mighty sovereign,   492
You have no cause to hold my friendship doubtful.
I never was, nor never will be false.

   K. Rich. Go, then, and muster men: but leave behind
Your son, George Stanley: look your heart be firm, 496

476 liege: *sovereign*   477 Welshman; *cf. n.*
479 mistrust; *cf. n.*

Or else his head's assurance is but frail.
 Stan. So deal with him as I prove true to you.
          Exit Stanley.

     Enter a Messenger.

 Mess. My gracious sovereign, now in Devonshire,
As I by friends am well advertised,   500
Sir Edward Courtney, and the haughty prelate,
Bishop of Exeter, his elder brother,
With many moe confederates are in arms.

    Enter another Messenger.

 [*Sec.*] *Mess.* In Kent, my liege, the Guildfords are
  in arms;   504
And every hour more competitors
Flock to the rebels, and their power grows strong.

    Enter another Messenger.

 [*Third*] *Mess.* My lord, the army of great Bucking-
  ham—
 K. Rich. Out on ye, owls! nothing but songs of
  death?   *He striketh him.* 508
There, take thou that, till thou bring better news.
 [*Third*] *Mess.* The news I have to tell your majesty
Is, that by sudden floods and fall of waters,
Buckingham's army is dispers'd and scatter'd; 512
And he himself wander'd away alone,
No man knows whither.
 K. Rich.   I cry thee mercy:
There is my purse, to cure that blow of thine.
Hath any well-advised friend proclaim'd   516
Reward to him that brings the traitor in?

---

497 assurance: *safety*   501 Sir Edward Courtney; *cf. n.*
502 Bishop of Exeter; *cf. n.*   503 moe: *more*
504 the Guildfords; *cf. n.*   505 competitors: *associates*
508 owls . . . death; *cf. n.*   513 *Cf. n.*

[*Third*] *Mess.* Such proclamation hath been made,
   my lord.

Enter another Messenger.

[*Fourth*] *Mess.* Sir Thomas Lovel, and Lord Mar-
   quess Dorset,
'Tis said, my liege, in Yorkshire are in arms: 520
But this good comfort bring I to your highness,
The Britaine navy is dispers'd by tempest.
Richmond, in Dorsetshire, sent out a boat
Unto the shore to ask those on the banks   524
If they were his assistants, yea or no;
Who answer'd him, they came from Buckingham
Upon his party: he, mistrusting them,
Hois'd sail, and made his course again for Britaine. 528
   K. Rich. March on, march on, since we are up in
      arms;
If not to fight with foreign enemies,
Yet to beat down these rebels here at home.

Enter Catesby.

   Cate. My liege, the Duke of Buckingham is
      taken,   532
That is the best news: that the Earl of Richmond
Is with a mighty power landed at Milford
Is colder news, but yet they must be told.
   K. Rich. Away towards Salisbury! while we reason
      here,   536
A royal battle might be won and lost.
Some one take order Buckingham be brought
To Salisbury; the rest march on with me.
                           Flourish. Exeunt.

522 tempest; *cf. n.*   528 Hois'd: *hoisted*
532 *Cf. n.*   534 landed; *cf. n.*

Scene Five

[The Same.   A Room in Lord Derby's House]

Enter Derby and Sir Christopher [Urswick].

Der. Sir Christopher, tell Richmond this from me:
That in the sty of the most deadly boar
My son, George Stanley, is frank'd up in hold:
If I revolt, off goes young George's head;   4
The fear of that holds off my present aid.
So, get thee gone: commend me to thy lord.
Withal, say that the queen hath heartily consented
He should espouse Elizabeth, her daughter.   8
But, tell me, where is princely Richmond now?
    Chris. At Pembroke, or at Ha'rford-west, in Wales.
    Der. What men of name resort to him?
    Chris. Sir Walter Herbert, a renowned soldier,   12
Sir Gilbert Talbot, Sir William Stanley,
Oxford, redoubted Pembroke, Sir James Blunt,
And Rice ap Thomas, with a valiant crew;
And many other of great name and worth: 16
And towards London do they bend their power,
If by the way they be not fought withal.
    Der. Well, hie thee to thy lord; I kiss his hand:
My letter will resolve him of my mind.   20
Farewell.   *Exeunt.*

3 frank'd up; *cf. n.*   in hold: *in custody as a hostage*
4 If I revolt; *cf. n.*   10 Ha'rford-west: *Haverfordwest*
12-15 *Cf. n.*   15 crew: *band*

ACT FIFTH

Scene One

[Salisbury.   An open Place]

*Enter Buckingham with [the Sheriff and] Halberds,
led to execution.*

    Buck. Will not King Richard let me speak with him?
    Sher. No, my good lord; therefore be patient.
    Buck. Hastings, and Edward's children, Grey and
      Rivers,
Holy King Henry, and thy fair son Edward,   4
Vaughan, and all that have miscarried
By underhand, corrupted, foul injustice,
If that your moody discontented souls
Do through the clouds behold this present hour,   8
Even for revenge mock my destruction!
This is All-Souls' day, fellow, is it not?
    Sher. It is.
    Buck. Why, then All-Souls' day is my body's dooms-
      day.   12
This is the day which, in King Edward's time,
I wish'd might fall on me, when I was found
False to his children and his wife's allies;
This is the day wherein I wish'd to fall   16
By the false faith of him whom most I trusted;
This, this All-Souls' day to my fearful soul
Is the determin'd respite of my wrongs.
That high All-Seer which I dallied with   20
Hath turn'd my feigned prayer on my head,
And given in earnest what I begg'd in jest.

10 All-Souls' day: *November first; cf. n.*   13 *Cf.* n.
19 determin'd . . . wrongs; *cf.* n.

Thus doth he force the swords of wicked men
To turn their own points in their masters' bosoms. 24
Thus Margaret's curse falls heavy on my neck:
'When he,' quoth she, 'shall split thy heart with sor-
    row,
Remember Margaret was a prophetess.'
Come, lead me, officers, to the block of shame: 28
Wrong hath but wrong, and blame the due of blame.
              Exeunt Buckingham with Officers.

Scene Two

[*A Plain near Tamworth*]

*Enter Richmond, Oxford, [Sir James] Blunt, [Sir
   Walter] Herbert, and Others, with drum and
   colours.*

  Richm. Fellows in arms, and my most loving friends,
Bruis'd underneath the yoke of tyranny,
Thus far into the bowels of the land
Have we march'd on without impediment: 4
And here receive we from our father Stanley
Lines of fair comfort and encouragement.
The wretched, bloody, and usurping boar,
That spoil'd your summer fields and fruitful vines, 8
Swills your warm blood like wash, and makes his
    trough
In your embowell'd bosoms, this foul swine
Is now even in the centry of this isle,
Near to the town of Leicester, as we learn: 12
From Tamworth thither is but one day's march.
In God's name, cheerly on, courageous friends,

24 bosoms; *cf. n.*   25 *Cf. n.*   3 bowels: *center*
6 Lines: *letters*   8 spoil'd: *despoiled; cf. n.*
10 embowell'd: *disemboweled*   11 centry: *exact center*

To reap the harvest of perpetual peace
By this one bloody trial of sharp war.   16
   Oxf. Every man's conscience is a thousand men,
To fight against this guilty homicide.
   Herb. I doubt not but his friends will turn to us.
   Blunt. He hath no friends but what are friends for
      fear,   20
Which in his dearest need will fly from him.
   Richm. All for our vantage: then, in God's name,
      march:
True hope is swift, and flies with swallow's wings;
Kings it makes gods, and meaner creatures kings.   24
                        Exeunt Omnes.

Scene Three

[*Bosworth Field*]

Enter King Richard in arms with [*the Duke of*]
  Norfolk, Ratcliff, and the Earl of Surrey.

   K. Rich. Here pitch our tent, even here in Bosworth
      field.
My Lord of Surrey, why look you so sad?
   Sur. My heart is ten times lighter than my looks.
   K. Rich. My Lord of Norfolk,—
   Nor.   Here, most gracious liege.   4
   K. Rich. Norfolk, we must have knocks; ha! must
      we not?
   Nor. We must both give and take, my loving lord.
   K. Rich. Up with my tent! here will I lie to-night;
      [*Soldiers begin to set up the King's tent.*]
But where to-morrow? Well, all's one for that.   8
Who hath descried the number of the traitors?

---

20 friends for fear; *cf. n.*
Scene Three S. d. Earl of Surrey; *cf. n.*   9 descried: *caught sight of*

Nor. Six or seven thousand is their utmost power.

K. Rich. Why, our battalia trebles that account;
Besides, the king's name is a tower of strength,   12
Which they upon the adverse faction want.
Up with the tent! Come, noble gentlemen,
Let us survey the vantage of the ground;
Call for some men of sound direction: 16
Let's lack no discipline, make no delay;
For lords, to-morrow is a busy day.   *Exeunt.*

*Enter [on the other side of the field,] Richmond, Sir
      William Brandon, Oxford, and Dorset.*

Richm. The weary sun hath made a golden set,
And, by the bright tract of his fiery car,   20
Gives token of a goodly day to-morrow.
Sir William Brandon, you shall bear my standard.
Give me some ink and paper in my tent:
I'll draw the form and model of our battle,   24
Limit each leader to his several charge,
And part in just proportion our small power.
My Lord of Oxford, you, Sir William Brandon,
And you, Sir Walter Herbert, stay with me.   28
The Earl of Pembroke keeps his regiment:
Good Captain Blunt, bear my good-night to him,
And by the second hour in the morning
Desire the earl to see me in my tent.   32
Yet one thing more, good captain, do for me;
Where is Lord Stanley quarter'd, do you know?

Blunt. Unless I have mista'en his colours much,—
Which, well I am assur'd, I have not done,—   36
His regiment lies half a mile at least

11 battalia: *battle array; cf. n.*   12 tower; *cf. n.*
16 direction: *capacity of directing*   18 S. d. Dorset; *cf. n.*
19 set: *setting*   20 tract: *trace, sunset glow*
25 Limit: *assign*   several charge: *individual command*
29 keeps: *stays with*

South from the mighty power of the king.

   Richm. If without peril it be possible,

Sweet Blunt, make some good means to speak with
   him,   40

And give him from me this most needful note.

   Blunt. Upon my life, my lord, I'll undertake it;

And so, God give you quiet rest to-night!

   Richm. Good-night, good Captain Blunt. Come,
   gentlemen,   44

Let us consult upon to-morrow's business.

In to my tent! the dew is raw and cold.

                          They withdraw into the tent.

  Enter Richard, Ratcliff, Norfolk, and Catesby.

   K. Rich. What is 't o'clock?

   Cate.   It's supper-time, my lord;

It's nine o'clock.

   K. Rich.   I will not sup to-night.   48

Give me some ink and paper.

What, is my beaver easier than it was,

And all my armour laid into my tent?

   Cate. It is, my liege; and all things are in readi-
   ness.   52

   K. Rich. Good Norfolk, hie thee to thy charge;

Use careful watch; choose trusty sentinels.

   Nor. I go, my lord.

   K. Rich. Stir with the lark to-morrow, gentle Norfolk.   56

   Nor. I warrant you, my lord.   *Exit.*

   K. Rich. Ratcliff!

   Rat. My lord?

   K. Rich.   Send out a pursuivant at arms

To Stanley's regiment; bid him bring his power   60

---

40 make . . . means: *contrive some opportunity*
41 needful: *important*   50 beaver: *face-guard of the helmet*

Before sun-rising, lest his son George fall
Into the blind cave of eternal night.
Fill me a bowl of wine.   Give me a watch.
Saddle white Surrey for the field to-morrow.   64
Look that my staves be sound, and not too heavy.
Ratcliff!
   Rat. My lord?
   K. Rich. Saw'st the melancholy Lord Northumber-
     land?   68
   Rat. Thomas the Earl of Surrey, and himself,
Much about cock-shut time, from troop to troop
Went through the army, cheering up the soldiers.
   K. Rich. So, I am satisfied.   Give me a bowl of
     wine: 72
I have not that alacrity of spirit,
Nor cheer of mind, that I was wont to have.
Set it down.   Is ink and paper ready?
   Rat. It is, my lord.   76
   K. Rich. Bid my guard watch; leave me.
Ratcliff, about the mid of night come to my tent
And help to arm me.   Leave me, I say.
             [King Richard retires into his tent.]
                 Exit Ratcliff [with Catesby].

*[Richmond's tent opens, and discovers him and his
          Officers, &c.]*

     Enter Derby to Richmond in his tent.

   Der. Fortune and victory sit on thy helm!   80
   Richm. All comfort that the dark night can afford
Be to thy person, noble father-in-law!
Tell me, how fares our noble mother?
   Der. I, by attorney, bless thee from thy mother,   84

62 blind: *dark*   63 watch: *sentinel* (?); *cf. n.*
65 staves: *lance-shafts*   68 Saw'st: *sawest thou*
70 cock-shut time: *evening twilight*   84 attorney: *proxy*

Who prays continually for Richmond's good:
So much for that. The silent hours steal on,
And flaky darkness breaks within the east.
In brief, for so the season bids us be,   88
Prepare thy battle early in the morning,
And put thy fortune to th' arbitrement
Of bloody strokes and mortal-staring war.
I, as I may,—that which I would I cannot,—   92
With best advantage will deceive the time,
And aid thee in this doubtful shock of arms:
But on thy side I may not be too forward,
Lest, being seen, thy brother, tender George,   96
Be executed in his father's sight.
Farewell: the leisure and the fearful time
Cuts off the ceremonious vows of love
And ample interchange of sweet discourse,   100
Which so long sunder'd friends should dwell upon:
God give us leisure for these rites of love!
Once more, adieu: be valiant, and speed well!
   Richm. Good lords, conduct him to his regiment. 104
I'll strive, with troubled noise, to take a nap,
Lest leaden slumber peise me down to-morrow,
When I should mount with wings of victory.
Once more, good-night, kind lords and gentlemen. 108
                        Exeunt. Manet Richmond.
O thou, whose captain I account myself,
Look on my forces with a gracious eye!
Put in their hands thy bruising irons of wrath,
That they may crush down with a heavy fall   112
Th' usurping helmets of our adversaries!
Make us thy ministers of chastisement,

87 flaky: *i.e. broken into flakes of cloud*   90 arbitrement: *decision*
91 mortal-staring: *fatal-visaged*
93 the time: *i.e. those who are about me*   96 tender George; *cf. n.*
98 leisure: *duration of opportunity*   105 troubled: *troublesome*
106 peise: *weigh*   111 bruising . . . wrath; *cf. n.*

That we may praise thee in thy victory!
To thee I do commend my watchful soul,   116
Ere I let fall the windows of mine eyes:
Sleeping and waking, O defend me still!   *Sleeps.*

*Enter the Ghost of Prince Edward, Son to Henry
the Sixth [between the two tents].*

 Ghost. To Richard. Let me sit heavy on thy soul
  to-morrow!
Think how thou stab'dst me in my prime of youth 120
At Tewkesbury: despair, therefore, and die!
 Ghost to Richmond. Be cheerful, Richmond; for the
  wronged souls
Of butcher'd princes fight in thy behalf:
King Henry's issue, Richmond, comforts thee.   124

Enter the Ghost of Henry the Sixth.

 Ghost. [To King Richard.] When I was mortal, my
  anointed body
By thee was punched full of [deadly] holes:
Think on the Tower and me; despair and die!
Henry the Sixth bids thee despair and die.   128
 To Richmond. Virtuous and holy, be thou conqueror!
Harry, that prophesied thou shouldst be king,
Doth comfort thee in sleep: live and flourish!

Enter the Ghost of Clarence.

 Ghost. [To King Richard.] Let me sit heavy in thy
  soul to-morrow!   132
I, that was wash'd to death with fulsome wine,
Poor Clarence, by thy guile betray'd to death!
To-morrow in the battle think on me,
And fall thy edgeless sword: despair, and die!   136

117 windows: *shutters*
133 fulsome: *nauseating*   119 *Cf. n.*

To Richmond. Thou offspring of the house of Lan-
     caster,
The wronged heirs of York do pray for thee:
Good angels guard thy battle! live, and flourish!

Enter the Ghosts of Rivers, Grey, and Vaughan.

[*Ghost of*] *Rivers.* [*To King Richard.*] Let me sit
     heavy in thy soul to-morrow,   140
Rivers, that died at Pomfret! despair, and die!
     [*Ghost of*] *Grey.* [*To King Richard.*] Think upon
     Grey, and let thy soul despair.
     [*Ghost of*] *Vaughan.* [*To King Richard.*] Think
     upon Vaughan, and with guilty fear
Let fall thy lance: despair, and die!—   144
     All to Richmond. Awake! and think our wrongs in
     Richard's bosom
Will conquer him! Awake, and win the day!

Enter the Ghost of Lord Hastings.

Ghost. [*To King Richard.*] Bloody and guilty,
     guiltily awake;
And in a bloody battle end thy days!   148
Think on Lord Hastings: despair, and die!—
     To Richmond. Quiet, untroubled soul, awake,
     awake!
Arm, fight, and conquer, for fair England's sake!

Enter the Ghosts of the two young Princes.

Ghosts. [*To King Richard.*] Dream on thy cousins
     smother'd in the Tower: 152
Let us be laid within thy bosom, Richard,
And weigh thee down to ruin, shame, and death!
Thy nephews' souls bid thee despair, and die!

144 lance; *cf. n.*   153 laid; *cf. n.*

To Richmond. Sleep, Richmond, sleep in peace, and
    wake in joy;   156
Good angels guard thee from the boar's annoy!
Live, and beget a happy race of kings!
Edward's unhappy sons do bid thee flourish.

Enter the Ghost of Anne, his wife.

Ghost. To Richard. Richard, thy wife, that wretched
    Anne, thy wife,   160
That never slept a quiet hour with thee,
Now fills thy sleep with perturbations:
To-morrow in the battle think on me,
And fall thy edgeless sword: despair, and die!   164
    To Richmond. Thou quiet soul, sleep thou a quiet
    sleep;
Dreams of success and happy victory!
Thy adversary's wife doth pray for thee.

Enter the Ghost of Buckingham.

Ghost. To Richard. The first was I that help'd thee
    to the crown;   168
The last was I felt thy tyranny.
O! in the battle think on Buckingham,
And die in terror of thy guiltiness!
Dream on, dream on, of bloody deeds and death: 172
Fainting, despair; despairing, yield thy breath!
    To Richmond. I died for hope ere I could lend thee
    aid:
But cheer thy heart, and be thou not dismay'd:
God and good angels fight on Richmond's side;   176
And Richard fall in height of all his pride!
                  [*The Ghosts vanish. King*] *Richard*
                        starts out of his dream.

157 annoy: *annoyance*   174 for hope; *cf. n.*

 K. Rich. Give me another horse! bind up my
  wounds!
Have mercy, Jesu! Soft! I did but dream.
O coward conscience, how dost thou afflict me! 180
The lights burn blue. It is now dead midnight.
Cold fearful drops stand on my trembling flesh.
What? do I fear myself? there's none else by:
Richard loves Richard; that is, I am I. 184
Is there a murtherer here? No. Yes, I am:
Then fly: what! from myself? Great reason: why?
Lest I revenge. What? myself upon myself?
Alack! I love myself. Wherefore? for any good 188
That I myself have done unto myself?
O no: alas! I rather hate myself
For hateful deeds committed by myself.
I am a villain. Yet I lie; I am not. 192
Fool, of thyself speak well: fool, do not flatter.
My conscience hath a thousand several tongues,
And every tongue brings in a several tale,
And every tale condemns me for a villain. 196
Perjury, [perjury,] in the high'st degree:
Murther, stern murther, in the dir'st degree;
All several sins, all us'd in each degree,
Throng all to the bar, crying all, 'Guilty! guilty!' 200
I shall despair. There is no creature loves me;
And if I die, no soul shall pity me:
Nay, wherefore should they, since that I myself
Find in myself no pity to myself? 204
Methought the souls of all that I had murther'd
Came to my tent; and every one did threat
To-morrow's vengeance on the head of Richard.

180 coward conscience; *cf. n.*
181 lights . . . blue; *cf. n.* now; *cf. n.*   183 *Cf. n.*
200 bar: *i.e. of justice*   202 shall; *cf. n.*

Enter Ratcliff.

Rat. My lord!   208

K. Rich. ['Zounds!] Who's there?

Rat. Ratcliff, my lord; 'tis I. The early village cock
Hath twice done salutation to the morn;
Your friends are up, and buckle on their armour. 212
   [*K. Rich.* O Ratcliff! I have dream'd a fearful
     dream.

What thinkest thou, will our friends prove all true?
   Rat. No doubt, my lord.]

   K. Rich.   O Ratcliff! I fear, I fear,—

   Rat. Nay, good my lord, be not afraid of
     shadows.   216

   K. Rich. By the apostle Paul, shadows to-night
Have struck more terror to the soul of Richard
Than can the substance of ten thousand soldiers,
Armed in proof, and led by shallow Richmond.   220
'Tis not yet near day. Come, go with me;
Under our tents I'll play the eaves-dropper,
To hear if any mean to shrink from me.

               Exeunt Richard and Ratcliff.

*Enter the Lords [Oxford and Others] to Richmond
sitting in his tent.*

   Lords. Good morrow, Richmond!   224

   Richm. Cry mercy, lords, and watchful gentlemen,
That you have ta'en a tardy sluggard here.

   Lords. How have you slept, my lord?

   Richm. The sweetest sleep, and fairest-boding
     dreams   228
That ever enter'd in a drowsy head,
Have I since your departure had, my lords.

---

209 'Zounds: *an oath, God's wounds*
220 proof: *impenetrable armor*
225 Cry mercy: *I beg your pardon*

213-215 *Cf. n.*
222 eaves-dropper; *cf. n.*

Methought their souls, whose bodies Richard mur-
    ther'd,
Came to my tent and cried on victory: 232
I promise you, my heart is very jocund
In the remembrance of so fair a dream.
How far into the morning is it, lords?
    Lords. Upon the stroke of four.   236
    Richm. Why, then 'tis time to arm and give direction.

His oration to his Soldiers.

More than I have said, loving countrymen,
The leisure and enforcement of the time
Forbids to dwell upon: yet remember this,   240
God and our good cause fight upon our side;
The prayers of holy saints and wronged souls,
Like high-rear'd bulwarks, stand before our faces;
Richard except, those whom we fight against   244
Had rather have us win than him they follow.
For what is he they follow? truly, gentlemen,
A bloody tyrant and a homicide;
One rais'd in blood, and one in blood establish'd;   248
One that made means to come by what he hath,
And slaughter'd those that were the means to help him;
A base foul stone, made precious by the foil
Of England's chair, where he is falsely set;   252
One that hath ever been God's enemy.
Then, if you fight against God's enemy,
God will in justice ward you as his soldiers;
If you do swear to put a tyrant down,   256
You sleep in peace, the tyrant being slain;
If you do fight against your country's foes,
Your country's fat shall pay your pains the hire;

232 cried on: *proclaimed; cf. n.*   238 *Cf. n.*
239 enforcement: *constraint, limitation*
244 except: *with the exception of*   255 ward: *guard*
256 swear; *cf. n.*   259 fat: *prosperity*

If you do fight in safeguard of your wives,   260
Your wives shall welcome home the conquerors;
If you do free your children from the sword,
Your children's children quits it in your age.
Then, in the name of God and all these rights,   264
Advance your standards, draw your willing swords.
For me, the ransom of my bold attempt
Shall be this cold corpse on the earth's cold face;
But if I thrive, the gain of my attempt   268
The least of you shall share his part thereof.
Sound drums and trumpets, boldly and cheerfully;
God and Saint George! Richmond and victory!

                                          Exeunt.

    Enter King Richard, Ratcliff, and Catesby
        [Attendants, and Forces].

  K. Rich. What said Northumberland as touching
    Richmond?   272
  Rat. That he was never trained up in arms.
  K. Rich. He said the truth: and what said Surrey
    then?
  Rat. He smil'd, and said, 'The better for our pur-
    pose.'
  K. Rich. He was in the right; and so, indeed, it
    is.   *Clock strikes.* 276
Tell the clock there. Give me a calendar.
Who saw the sun to-day?
  Rat.   Not I, my lord.
  K. Rich. Then he disdains to shine; for by the book
He should have brav'd the east an hour ago: 280
A black day will it be to somebody.
Ratcliff!

265 Advance: *raise*   266 ransom: *forfeit*
277 Tell: *count the strokes of*   279 book: *i.e. the calendar*
280 brav'd: *made splendid*

Rat. My lord?

   K. Rich.   The sun will not be seen to-day;
The sky doth frown and lower upon our army.   284
I would these dewy tears were from the ground.
Not shine to-day! Why, what is that to me
More than to Richmond? for the self-same heaven
That frowns on me looks sadly upon him.   288

Enter Norfolk.

   Nor. Arm, arm, my lord! the foe vaunts in the field.

   K. Rich. Come, bustle, bustle; caparison my horse.
Call up Lord Stanley, bid him bring his power:
I will lead forth my soldiers to the plain,   292
And thus my battle shall be ordered:
My forward shall be drawn [out all] in length,
Consisting equally of horse and foot;
Our archers shall be placed in the midst: 296
John Duke of Norfolk, Thomas Earl of Surrey,
Shall have the leading of the foot and horse.
They thus directed, we will follow
In the main battle, whose puissance on either side 300
Shall be well winged with our chiefest horse.
This, and Saint George to boot! What think'st thou,
    Norfolk?

   Nor. A good direction, warlike sovereign.
This found I on my tent this morning.   304
'Jockey of Norfolk, be not so bold,
For Dickon thy master is bought and sold.'

   K. Rich. A thing devised by the enemy!
Go, gentlemen; every man to his charge: 308

---

289 vaunts: *boasts*   290 caparison: *put trappings on*
301 winged: *flanked*   303 direction: *order of battle*
305 Jockey; *cf. n.*
306 Dickon: *a cognomen of the Devil, with a quibble on the nick-*
    name 'Dick' for Richard   bought and sold: *i.e. betrayed for*
    a bribe   *

Let not our babbling dreams affright our souls;
For conscience is a word that cowards use,
Devis'd at first to keep the strong in awe:
Our strong arms be our conscience, swords our law. 312
March on, join bravely, let us to 't pell-mell;
If not to heaven, then hand in hand to hell.

[*His oration to his Army.*]

What shall I say more than I have inferr'd?
Remember whom you are to cope withal: 316
A sort of vagabonds, rascals, and run-aways,
A scum of Britaines and base lackey peasants,
Whom their o'ercloyed country vomits forth
To desperate adventures and assur'd destruction. 320
You sleeping safe, they bring you to unrest;
You having lands, and bless'd with beauteous wives,
They would restrain the one, distain the other.
And who doth lead them but a paltry fellow,   324
Long kept in Britaine at our mother's cost?
A milksop, one that never in his life
Felt so much cold as over shoes in snow?
Let's whip these stragglers o'er the seas again;   328
Lash hence these overweening rags of France,
These famish'd beggars, weary of their lives;
Who, but for dreaming on this fond exploit,
For want of means, poor rats, had hang'd them-
    selves: 332
If we be conquer'd, let men conquer us,
And not these bastard Britaines; whom our fathers
Have in their own land beaten, bobb'd, and thump'd,
And, on record, left them the heirs of shame.   336
Shall these enjoy our lands? lie with our wives?

315 *Cf. n.*   316 cope withal: *have to do with*   317 sort: *set*
323 distain: *defile*   325 Britaine: *Brittany*
329 overweening: *presumptuous*   335 bobb'd: *banged*

Ravish our daughters?   *Drum afar off.*
                          Hark! I hear their drum.
Fight, gentlemen of England! fight, bold yeomen!
Draw, archers, draw your arrows to the head!   340
Spur your proud horses hard, and ride in blood;
Amaze the welkin with your broken staves!

                    Enter a Messenger.

What says Lord Stanley? will he bring his power?
   Mess. My lord, he doth deny to come.   344
   K. Rich. Off with his son George's head!
   Nor. My lord, the enemy is pass'd the marsh:
After the battle let George Stanley die.
   K. Rich. A thousand hearts are great within my
      bosom: 348
Advance our standards! set upon our foes!
Our ancient word of courage, fair Saint George,
Inspire us with the spleen of fiery dragons!
Upon them! Victory sits upon our helms.   352
                                          [*Exeunt.*]

                         Scene Four

                 [*Another Part of the Field*]

         *Alarum: Excursions. Enter [Norfolk and
                 Forces; to him] Catesby.*

   Cate. Rescue, my Lord of Norfolk! rescue, rescue!
The king enacts more wonders than a man,
Daring an opposite to every danger:
His horse is slain, and all on foot he fights,   4
Seeking for Richmond in the throat of death.
Rescue, fair lord, or else the day is lost!

344 deny: *refuse*   345 *Cf. n.*   346 marsh; *cf. n.*
351 spleen: *wrath*   3 opposite: *adversary*

Alarums.   Enter Richard.

  K. Rich. A horse! a horse! my kingdom for a horse!
  Cate. Withdraw, my lord; I'll help you to a horse. 8
  K. Rich. Slave! I have set my life upon a cast,
And I will stand the hazard of the die.
I think there be six Richmonds in the field;
Five have I slain to-day, instead of him.—   12
A horse! a horse! my kingdom for a horse!

                                 [Exeunt.]

Alarum.   Enter Richard and Richmond.   They fight;
    Richard is slain.   Retreat and flourish.   Enter
    Richmond, Derby bearing the crown, with divers
    other Lords.

  Richm. God and your arms be prais'd, victorious
    friends:
The day is ours, the bloody dog is dead.
  Der. Courageous Richmond, well hast thou acquit
    thee!   16
Lo! here, this long-usurped royalty
From the dead temples of this bloody wretch
Have I pluck'd off, to grace thy brows withal:
Wear it, [enjoy it,] and make much of it.   20
  Richm. Great God of heaven, say amen to all!
But, tell me, is young George Stanley living?
  Der. He is, my lord, and safe in Leicester town;
Whither, if you please, we may withdraw us.   24
  Richm. What men of name are slain on either side?
  Der. John Duke of Norfolk, Walter Lord Ferrers,
Sir Robert Brakenbury, and Sir William Brandon.
  Richm. Inter their bodies as become their births: 28

---

7 *Cf. n.*   9 cast: *i.e. of the dice, a gambler's chance*
10 hazard: *chance*   11 six Richmonds; *cf. n.*
16 acquit: *acquitted*   17 royalty; *cf. n.*
27 Brandon; *cf. n.*

Proclaim a pardon to the soldiers fled
That in submission will return to us;
And then, as we have ta'en the sacrament,
We will unite the white rose and the red: 32
Smile, heaven, upon this fair conjunction,
That long have frown'd upon their enmity!
What traitor hears me, and says not amen?
England hath long been mad, and scarr'd herself;   36
The brother blindly shed the brother's blood,
The father rashly slaughter'd his own son,
The son, compell'd, been butcher to the sire:
All this divided York and Lancaster,   40
Divided in their dire division,
O, now let Richmond and Elizabeth,
The true succeeders of each royal house,
By God's fair ordinance conjoin together;   44
And let their heirs—God, if thy will be so,—
Enrich the time to come with smooth-fac'd peace,
With smiling plenty, and fair prosperous days!
Abate the edge of traitors, gracious Lord,   48
That would reduce these bloody days again,
And make poor England weep in streams of blood!
Let them not live to taste this land's increase,
That would with treason wound this fair land's
          peace!   52
Now civil wounds are stopp'd, peace lives again:
That she may long live here, God say amen! *Exeunt.*

38, 39 *Cf. n.*   45 their; *cf. n*
48 Abate: *blunt*

FINIS.

NOTES

I. i. 1. *winter . . . York.* Alluding to the cognizance of Edward IV, which was *a sun,* in memory of the *three suns,* which are said to have appeared at the battle which he gained over the Lancastrians at Mortimer's Cross, 1461. See *Holinshed,* iii. 660. There is also a quibble on 'son' and 'sun.' The early texts all have 'son'; modern editors adopt the emendation 'sun.'

I. i. 12. *He capers.* I.e. War, first personified as a rough soldier, now 'capers.'

I. i. 15. *amorous.* A looking-glass that reflects a face fond of itself (Schmidt). Cf. however, 'lascivious pleasing of a lute' (13); that is, as Furness suggests, the looking-glass and the lute may be interpreted as active agents.

I. i. 19. *feature.* Denoted the whole exterior personal appearance (Wright).

dissembling. Fraudful, deceitful (Johnson). There is some disagreement with this interpretation.

I. i. 24. *weak piping time of peace.* I.e. because in times of peace the loud, stirring strains of martial music are no longer heard. Cf. *Much Ado About Nothing,* II. iii. 13-15: 'I have known, when there was no music with him but the drum and fife; and now had he rather hear the tabor and the pipe.'

I. i. 29. *fair well-spoken days.* Cf. *Twelfth Night,* II. iv. 6: 'Of these most brisk and giddy-paced times'; *Timon of Athens,* IV. iii. 495: 'Strange times, that weep with laughing, not with weeping.'

I. i. 30. *I am determined to prove a villain.* It is perhaps possible, as Charles Lamb suggests, that Richard uses villain here in the sense of 'churl' as opposed to 'courtier,' and not in our modern sense of 'wicked man.' On the other hand, cf. *3 Henry VI,* V. vi. 78, 79: 'Then, since the heavens have shap'd my

body so, Let hell make crook'd my mind to answer it.'
Lamb's suggestion is unnecessarily apologetic.

I. i. 33. *By drunken prophecies.* I.e. by inventing
prophecies for drunken men to spread abroad.

I. i. 36. *true and just.* I.e. and therefore the less
likely to entertain any suspicion (Wright).

I. i. 39, 40. *About a prophecy, which says that G Of
Edward's heirs the murtherer shall be.* '[Clarence's
death] rose of a foolish prophesie, which was, that,
after K. Edward, one should reigne, whose first letter
of his name should be a G.' *Holinshed, iii. 703. Halle,*
326.

I. i. 43. *His majesty.* An anachronism. The title
used by Edward IV was 'most high and mighty prince'
(Bradley).

I. i. 55. *cross-row.* Christ-cross-row. The alphabet was so called from the figure of the cross formerly
prefixed to it (Murray: N.E.D.).

I. i. 65. *tempers.* The reading of the Folio is 'That
tempts him to this harsh extremity.' Most recent editors prefer here the reading of the Quarto. On the
other hand Qq. 5-8 agree with the Folio in reading
'tempts.' 'Harsh' is found only in the Folio.

I. i. 67. *Anthony Woodville,* Earl Rivers, eldest
brother to the Queen of Edward IV, appointed gov-
ernor to the Prince of Wales. See note on II. i. 68.

I. i. 72. *night-walking heralds.* Ironical description of the messengers busied with the king's illicit
business (Furness).

I. i. 73. *Mistress Shore.* Jane Shore was famous
as the mistress of Edward IV. She was the daughter
of a Cheapside mercer and the wife of a goldsmith in
Lombard Street. She died in poverty c. 1527. See
the tragedy by Nicholas Rowe, *Jane Shore.*

I. i. 75. *Lord Hastings was for her delivery.* The
Quarto reads 'Lord Hastings was to her for his de-

livery.' The Quarto reading here is more obvious, but
feebler.

I. i. 81. *The jealous o'erworn widow*. Elizabeth
Woodville was born in 1437, so that her age at this
time would be at least about forty. She had been
married before she became Edward's wife, a fact
which seems to intensify Richard's hate. Cf. line 92
below, which does not confirm the accusation of
jealousy.

I. i. 88. *an't*. Pope's modernization has been followed in preference to the 'and' of the early editions.

I. i. 106. *abjects*. 'outcasts,' the more usual sense,
is perhaps the meaning here. Cf. also *Henry VIII.*
I. i. 126, 127: 'and his eye revil'd Me, as his abject
object.'

I. i. 109. *widow*. The word is used contemptuously, as in 81 above. I.e. the Widow Grey, whom
King Edward IV has taken to wife.

I. i. 115. *lie for you*. With probably a quibble on
the other meaning of 'lie.'

I. i. 133. *play*. The reading of the Quarto is 'prey.'

I. i. 138. *Saint John*. Quarto, 'Saint Paul.' Elsewhere in the play Richard's favorite oath is by Saint
Paul.

I. ii. 1. *Anne*. The historical Lady Anne did not
attend Henry VI's funeral; and the dialogue between
her and Richard is Shakespeare's invention. 'The
dead corps, on the Ascension euen [May 22, 1471],
was conueied with billes and glaues pompouslie . . .
from the Tower to the church of saint Paule, and
there, laid on a beire or coffen bare faced, the same in
presence of the beholders did bleed: where it rested
the space of one whole daie. From thense he was
caried to the Blackfriers . . .: and, on the next daie
after, it was conueied in a boat . . . vnto the monas-

terie of Chertseie. . . .' *Holinshed,* iii. 690. Richard
married Anne in 1472.

I. ii. 19. *wolves.* The reading of the Quarto is
'adders,' which some editors hold to be more con-
sistent with the meaning of the passage.

I. ii. 29. Chertsey is in Surrey.

I. ii. 56. *Open their congeal'd mouths and bleed
afresh.* Referring to the belief that a murdered body
will bleed afresh in the presence of the murderer. See
note on I. ii. 1. above.

I. ii. 76. *crimes.* The reading of the Quarto is
'evils.' Many editors adopt the Quarto reading to
maintain the parallelism of lines 75-77 and 78-80.

I. ii. 78. *diffus'd.* The Quarto reading of this line
is 'defus'd infection of a man'; F1, 'defus'd infection
of man; F3, F4, 'diffus'd infection of a man.' There
have been many conjectures concerning the exact
meaning of 'defus'd.' See, however, *King Lear,* I. iv.
2: 'That can my speech diffuse'; and *Merry Wives of
Windsor,* IV. iv. 56: 'With some diffused song.'

I. ii. 92. *slain by Edward's hand.* Cf. *3 Henry VI,*
V. v. 38-40 in which the killing is portrayed; *Holinshed,* iii. 688.

I. ii. 103. *hedge-hog.* Applied to Richard because
of its hump-backed appearance, with a pun on Richard's heraldic emblem, the boar (hog).

I. ii. 148. *poison on a fouler toad.* Toads were
believed to be venomous.

I. ii. 151. *basilisks.* Fabulous reptiles, also called
cockatrices, alleged to be hatched by a serpent from
a cock's eggs; ancient authors stated that their hissing
drove away all other serpents, and that their breath,
or even their look, was fatal (Murray. N.E.D.).

I. ii. 158. *Rutland.* For an account of his murder
see *3 Henry VI,* I. iii.

I. ii. 213. *Crosby House* fronted on Bishopsgate
Street Within. It was built by Sir John Crosby in

1466, and later Richard, when lord protector, was lodged there.

I. ii. 228. *White-Friars*. According to Holinshed the body was conveyed to Blackfriars. See note on I. ii. 1 above.

I. ii. 229, 230. Cf. *Titus Andronicus*, II. i. 82, 83: 'She is a woman, therefore may be woo'd; She is a woman, therefore may be won.'

I. ii. 242. *three months since*. Tewkesbury was fought on May 4; Henry was buried on May 23, 1471.

I. iii. 12. *the trust of Richard Gloucester*. '. . . the duke of Glocester bare him in open sight so reuerentlie to the prince . . . that at the councell next assembled he was made the onelie man, chosen and thought most meet to be protector of the king and his realme; so that (were it destinie or were it follie) the lambe was betaken to the woolfe to keepe.' *Holinshed*, iii. 716. *More*, 22/31. The historical date of Richard's appointment is April or May, 1483.

I. iii. 15. *determin'd, not concluded yet*. I.e. it has been decided on, but has not yet been made official.

I. iii. 16 S. d. *Derby*. Thomas, Lord Stanley, was not created Earl of Derby until 1485. Shakespeare has either confused this Lord Stanley with Sir William Stanley, or thought Thomas, Lord Stanley, later the Earl of Derby, two different men. In the Folio he is called Stanley during the third, fourth, and fifth acts.

I. iii. 20. *Countess Richmond*. Margaret Beaufort, daughter of the Duke of Somerset. She married in 1455 Edmund Tudor, Earl of Richmond. She married next Lord Henry Stafford, and her third husband was Thomas, Lord Stanley. See preceding note.

I. iii. 114-116. The Folio omits 114; the Quarto, 116.

I. iii. 121. *Ere you were queen, ay, or your husband king*. Edward became king in 1460 when Richard was

eight years old. The 2d and 3d parts of *Henry VI*
similarly give him a prominent part in Edward's early
struggles.

I. iii. 128.   *factious for the house of Lancaster.* Cf.
3 Henry VI, III. ii. 6, in which it is stated that Sir
John Grey died 'in quarrel of the house of York.' The
statement of Richard that Sir John was a Lancastrian
is historically correct.

I. iii. 130.   *Margaret's battle.* Margaret was victorious at St. Albans in the battle of Bernard's Heath
on Feb. 17, 1461. Some editors, however, believe that
'battle' here has the meaning of 'army.'

I. iii. 160-162.   The structure of these lines is confused. They may be paraphrased as follows: Which
of you who looks at me does not tremble, if not because, as subjects, you bow before your queen, then
since, as rebels, you quake before the sovereign you
have deposed?

I. iii. 167.   Margaret fled into France in 1464 after
the battle of Hexham. Edward issued a proclamation
forbidding her to return. On April 14, 1471, she
landed at Weymouth. After the battle of Tewkesbury
she was confined in the Tower until 1475. In 1476
she again went to France, after which time she did
not return to England. She died in 1482. The historical time of the present scene is 1483, hence her introduction here is dramatic fiction.

I. iii. 174.   *The curse my noble father laid on thee.*
Cf. *3 Henry VI,* I. iv. 164-166: 'There, take the crown,
and with the crown my curse, And in thy need such
comfort come to thee As now I reap at thy too cruel
hand!'

I. iii. 187.   *Northumberland.* Sir Henry Percy,
third Earl of Northumberland, killed at Towton, 1461.
Cf. *3 Henry VI,* I. iv. 150-151; 169-174.

I. iii. 228.   *elvish-mark'd.* A disfigurement given
by the elves to a child at birth.

I. iii. 228. *rooting hog.* Richard's badge was a white boar. In the second year of Richard's reign, 1484, William Collingborne published the couplet:

> 'The Cat, the Rat, and Louell our dog,
> Rule all England vnder an hog.

Meaning by the hog, the dreadfull wild boare, which was the kings cognisance.' *Holinshed,* iii. 746. *Halle,* 398. Collingborne was executed for this indiscretion.

I. iii. 256. *Your fire-new stamp of honour is scarce current.* The figure of speech is from the art of coining or minting money. 'Fire-new' = newly coined. Dorset's title was granted him on April 18, 1475 (*Stow,* 713. *Holinshed,* iii. 702). He had therefore held this title for about eight years.

I. iii. 277. *My charity is outrage, life my shame.* I.e. outrage is the only charity shown me, and my life is my shame.

I. iii. 285, 286. *curses never pass The lips of those that breathe them in the air.* A possible reference to an old belief that curses to be efficacious should be uttered within walls. More probably the meaning is: 'curses never take effect outside the lips of those who utter them' (Tawney).

I. iii. 321. The Quarto reading is 'you my noble Lord.' Capell's emendation 'you, my noble lords' is accepted by many editors.

I. iii. 333. *Dorset.* In the Quarto the name appears as Vaughan. Spedding remarked (p. 85) that he could see no reason for the change. Pickersgill in reply (p. 11) points out that later it is upon Rivers, Vaughan, and Grey that Richard's vengeance falls. Nearly all editors accept the reading 'Vaughan.'

I. iii. 353. *millstones.* Probably a proverbial expression. Cf. *Troilus and Cressida,* I. ii. 156: 'Hecuba laughed that her eyes ran o'er.'—'With millstones.'

I. iv. S. d. In the Quarto Brakenbury and the

Keeper are the same person. In the Folio Brakenbury does not enter until after line 75. It is possible
that the Quarto text represents an acting version in
which an extra character was omitted for economical
reasons.

I. iv. 10. *Burgundy*. Clarence, when a child, had
resided under Burgundian protection at Utrecht, the
Netherlands being then a part of the domains of the
Dukes of Burgundy.

I. iv. 45. *melancholy flood*. I.e. the river Styx,
across which Charon, the 'sour ferryman,' conveys in
his boat the souls of the newly dead into 'the kingdom
of perpetual night,' i.e. Hades.

I. iv. 49. *father-in-law*. Clarence married Isabel
Neville, the elder daughter of Warwick.

I. iv. 50. *What scourge for perjury*. Cf. *3 Henry
VI*, V. i. 106.

I. iv. 53. *A shadow like an angel*. I.e. the ghost of
Edward, Prince of Wales, son of Henry VI.

I. iv. 56. *That stabb'd me in the field by Tewkesbury*. Cf. *3 Henry VI*, V. v. 40, in which the killing
is portrayed.

I. iv. 160.   *costard*. A species of large apple.
The term was a vulgar colloquialism for the head.

I. iv. 163.   *sop*. A grim jest of the murderer. It
was the custom to sop bread in wine. Probably there
is also implied a quibble on 'milk-sop.'

I. iv. 199. This line is omitted in the Folio. The
preceding half line in the Quarto is 'to have redemp-
tion.' Probably the Folio omits the line in accordance
with the statute of 1606 against blasphemy.

I. iv. 230. *gallant-springing*. I.e. blooming Plantagenet; a prince in the spring of life (Johnson).

I. iv. 252. *snow in harvest*. Cf. *Proverbs*, xxvi, 1:
'As snow in summer, and as rain in harvest, so honour
is not seemly for a fool.'

I. iv. 280. *malmsey-butt*. '. . . the duke was cast

into the Tower, and therewith adiudged for a traitor, and priuilie drowned in a butt of malmesie, the eleuenth of March, in the beginning of the seuententh yeare of the kings reigne.' *Holinshed*, iii. 703. The earlier portion of this scene is Shakespeare's invention.

I. iv. 282. *Pilate*. Cf. *Richard II*, IV. i. 239: 'Though some of you with Pilate wash your hands.'

II. i. 2. *united league*. 'But [King Edward], in his last sicknesse, when he perceiued his naturall strength so sore infeebled, that he despaired all recouerie . . . called some of them before him that were at variance, and in especiall the lord marquesse Dorset, the queenes sonne by hir first husband. So did he also William the lord Hastings.' The lords, Holinshed then tells us, 'ech forgaue other, and ioined their hands togither; when (as it after appeared by their deeds) their hearts were farre asunder.' *Holinshed*, iii. 713, 714. *More*, 8/15.

II. i. 7. *Rivers and Hastings*. The Folio has 'Dorset and Rivers,' but these two were nephew and uncle, both belonging to the queen's party. Line 25 below shows that the reading of the Quarto is, in this instance, the correct one. See also note on l. 68 below.

II. i. 11. *So thrive I, as I truly swear the like*. I.e. May my fortune be in accordance with the truth of my oath. See also line 16 and line 24 below.

II. i. 14, 15. *award Either of you to be the other's end*. I.e. cause each to die by the other's agency [either of you to suffer the other's end]. A prophetic warning. See III. iii. 14.

II. i. 66. *Of you, and you, Lord Rivers, and of Dorset*. The Quarto reading is: 'Of you, Lord Rivers, and Lord Grey, of you.' It is Grey later who is associated in death with Rivers.

II. i. 68. *Lord Woodville, and Lord Scales*. The

Quarto omits this line. Woodville was the Lord Rivers
addressed in line 66, and he was also Lord Scales in
right of his wife, the heir and daughter of Lord Scales.
Shakespeare was apparently misled into thinking
Rivers three separate persons by the passage in Halle,
347: 'The gouernance of this younge Prince was committed too lord Antony Wooduile erle Ryuers and
lord Scales, brother to the quene.' He was unaware
that one person bore all three of these titles. See also
Holinshed, iii. 714, a passage possible to misinterpret
in the same way. See note on II. ii. 149.

II. i. 69-72. Cf. Milton's *Eikonoklastes* (1649),
chap. 1, in which, in illustrating that 'the deepest
policy of a tyrant hath been ever to counterfeit religious,' Milton states that the poets 'have been in this
point so mindful of decorum, as to put never more
pious words in the mouth of any person, than of a
tyrant. I shall not instance an abstruse author . . .,
but one whom we well know was the closest companion
of these his [i.e., King Charles'] solitudes, William
Shakespeare; who introduces the person of Richard
the Third, speaking in as high a strain of piety and
mortification as is uttered in any passage of this book
[*Eikon Basilike*], and sometimes to the same sense
and purpose with some words in this place: "I intended," saith he, "not only to oblige my friends, but
my enemies."'

II. i. 104. *give pardon to a slave.* '. . . although
king Edward were consenting to his death, yet he
much did both lament his infortunate chance, & repent
his sudden execution: insomuch that, when anie person sued to him for the pardon of malefactors con-
demned to death, he would accustomablie saie, &
openlie speake: "Oh infortunate brother, for whose
life not one would make sute!"' *Holinshed,* iii. 703.
Halle, 362.

II. i. 113. *Oxford.* John de Vere, thirteenth Earl

of Oxford (1443-1513) fled to France before the battle of Tewkesbury was fought. Cf., however, *3 Henry VI*, V. v. 2.

II. ii. 6. *Castaways.* Persons lost or abandoned by Providence. Cf. *I Corinthians,* ix, 17: 'I myself should be a castaway.'

II. ii. 24. For 'pitied me' the Quarto reads 'hugd me in his arme.'

II. ii. 40. *Edward.* The Duchess and her grand-children speak of Clarence's death (February, 1478) as recent. Queen Elizabeth next enters distracted with grief for the loss of King Edward (April 9, 1483).

II. ii. 70. The precise meaning of this passage has been disputed. The general sense is as follows: Elizabeth says that so great have been her griefs that her eyes may be compared to the sea, governed by the influence of the moon, which receives back from the rivers the moisture which it gives forth.

II. ii. 80. *The mother of these griefs.* I.e. by her years and position, the chief mourner of all.

II. ii. 117. *broken rancour.* The structure of this passage is confused, but the general meaning clear. It may be paraphrased as follows: 'Your late quarrels, which, swollen high, had broken out in rancor, are now knit and joined together, and this healing of your quarrels must be preserved and cherished.'

II. ii. 120. *little train.* '. . . the duke of Glocester, vnderstanding that the lords, which at that time were about the king, intended to bring him vp to his corona-tion accompanied with such power of their freends, that it should be hard for him to bring his purpose to passe, without the gathering and great assemblie of people and in maner of open warre, whereof the end (he wist) was doubtfull; and in which, the king being on their side, his part should haue the face and name of a rebellion: he secretlie therfore by diuers means caused the queene to be persuaded and brought in

the mind, that it neither were need, and also should
be ieopardous, the king to come vp strong.' *Holinshed,*
iii. 714. *More,* 14/6.

II. ii. 121. *Ludlow.* 'As soone as the king was departed, the noble prince his sonne drew toward London; which at the time of his decease kept his hous-
hold at Ludlow in Wales. . . .' *Holinshed,* iii. 714.
More, 12/6.

II. ii. 149. *queen's proud kindred.* 'To the gouernance and ordering of this yoong prince, at his sending
thither, was there appointed sir Anthonie Wooduile,
lord Riuers, and brother vnto the queene; a right
honourable man, as valiant of hand as politike in
counsell. Adioined were vnto him other of the same
partie; and in effect euerie one as he was neerest of
kin vnto the queene, so was he planted next about the
prince. That drift by the queene now vnwiselie deuised, whereby hir bloud might of youth be rooted into
the princes fauour, the duke of Glocester turned vnto
their destruction; and vpon that ground set the foun-
dation of all his vnhappie building.' *Holinshed,* iii.
714. *More,* 12/6.

II. iii. 4. *seldom comes the better.* A proverbial
saying. '. . . began there, here and there abouts,
some maner of muttering among the people, as though
all should not long be well, though they neither wist
what they feared, nor wherefore: were it, that, before
such great things, mens hearts of a secret instinct of
nature misgiue them; as the sea without wind swelleth
of himselfe sometime before a tempest. . . .' *Holinshed,* iii. 721. *More,* 43/19.

II. iii. 11. *Woe to that land that's govern'd by a
child.* Cf. *Ecclesiastes,* x, 16: 'Woe to thee, O land,
when thy king is a child.'

II. iii. 17. *nine months.* Henry VI was proclaimed
king at Paris in October, 1422, when he was about

a year old. His coronation at Paris did not take place until 1430, when he was about nine years old.

II. iv. 1. *Stony-Stratford*. The Quarto reverses the order of the towns, putting Northampton first. The Prince was on his way from Ludlow to London. Stony-Stratford is nearer London than Northampton. The Folio reading, as pointed out by Pickersgill, is in accordance with Halle's *Chronicle*. The Prince was taken back to Northampton. See also *Holinshed*, iii. 715/1/48. *More*, 16/20; 18/7.

II. iv. 28. *he could gnaw a crust at two hours old*. Cf. *3 Henry VI*, V. vi. 53, 54: 'Teeth hadst thou in thy head when thou wast born, To signify thou cams 't to bite the world.'

II. iv. 37. *Pitchers have ears*. A proverbial saying, 'small pitchers have great ears.' Cf. *Taming of the Shrew*, IV. iv. 52: 'Pitchers have ears. . . .'

II. iv. 37. S. d. The Quarto assigns the part of the Messenger to Dorset, probably to avoid the introduction of another actor. The reception of the Messenger and the tone of his speeches indicate that the Folio is here correct.

II. iv. 54. *map*. Possibly this word is here used in an astrological sense meaning a horoscope of future events.

II. iv. 66. *we will to sanctuary*. Certain buildings belonging to ecclesiastical foundations, as well as churches, were privileged for criminals and other persons in danger of their lives. ' [Queen Elizabeth] in great fright & heauinesse, bewailing hir childes reigne, hir freends mischance, and hir owne infortune, damning the time that euer she dissuaded the gathering of power about the king, gat hir selfe in all the hast possible with hir yoonger sonne and hir daughters out of the palace of Westminster, (in which she then laie,) into the sanctuarie; lodging hir selfe and hir companie

there in the abbats place.' *Holinshed*, iii. 715. *More*,
19/1.

III. i. S. d. *Cardinal.* According to *More*, 25/28
(Holinshed's authority), the Cardinal who undertook
the mission of bringing the Duke of York out of
sanctuary was Rotherham, Archbishop of York. In
Halle, 352, the Cardinal of Act III, sc. i, is Bourchier,
Archbishop of Canterbury. Critics are divided in opinion as to whether Shakespeare intended to present
more than one personage.

III. i. 16. ' "What my brother marquesse hath
donne I cannot saie, but in good faith I dare well answer for mine vncle Riuers and my brother here, that
they be innocent of anie such matter." ' *Holinshed*,
iii. 715. *More*, 17/31.

III. i. 17 S. d. 'When the king approched neere
to the citie, Edmund Shaw, goldsmith, then maior,
with William White, and Iohn Matthew, shiriffes,
and all the other aldermen in scarlet, with fiue hundred horsse of the citizens, in violet, receiued him
reuerentlie at Harnesie; and riding from thence accompanied him into the citie, which he entered the
fourth daie of Maie, the first and last yeare of his
reigne.' *Holinshed*, iii. 716. *More*, 22/24.

III. i. 36. *pluck him perforce.* Richard, after ad-
vising that 'my lord cardinall' be sent to fetch the
Duke of York out of sanctuary, added, 'And if she be
percase so obstinate, and so preciselie set vpon hir
owne will . . . then shall we, by mine aduise, by the
kings authoritie, fetch him out of that prison. . . .'
Holinshed. iii. 717. *More*, 24/25.

III. i. 40, 41. *God [in heaven] forbid We should infringe the holy privilege Of blessed sanctuary.* 'God
forbid that anie man should, for anie thing earthlie,
enterprise to breake the immunitie & libertie of the
sacred sanctuarie. . . .' *Holinshed*, iii. 717. *More*,

26/16. See also *Holinshed,* iii. 718, for the substance of the arguments used by Buckingham in ii. 48-56: Cf. 'And verilie, I haue often heard of sanctuarie men, but I neuer heard earst of sanctuarie children.' *Holinshed,* supra.

III. i. 46. *Weigh it but with the grossness of this age.* The meaning seems to be that the present age is not one to stand on the mere technicalities of a situation when the person seeking sanctuary has no reason to claim it.

III. i. 56. *children.* Buckingham sets up the presumption that children could not commit crimes, and, therefore, could have no reason to seek sanctuary. See note on line 40 above.

III. i. 65. *the Tower.* The Duke of York left sanctuary on June 16, 1483. *Excerpta Historica,* 16, 17. Edward V was already in the Tower on May 19. *Grants,* viii. 15. Shakespeare follows the account in *Holinshed,* iii. 721. *More,* 41/2.

III. i. 69. *Did Julius Cæsar build that place.* The Tower is traditionally said to have been built by Julius Cæsar. The Norman Keep is to-day sometimes called Cæsar's Tower, although its official name is The White Tower, and it was built by William the Conqueror circa 1078. See Stow, *Survey,* ed. Morley, p. 73.

III. i. 79. *So wise so young, they say, do never live long.* A proverbial saying. 'They be of short life who are of wit so pregnant' (Timothy Bright: *A Treatise of Melancholie,* 1586).

III. i. 82. *the formal Vice, Iniquity.* A reference to the old morality plays in which the Vice (comic demon) was sometimes called Iniquity. Richard says that he will speak equivocally, like the Vice of the old play, and thus to one word give a double meaning. Fame may live long, but one person of whom he is thinking will not.

III. i. 97. *dear.* This is probably a misprint for 'dread,' the reading of the Quarto.

III. i. 131. *you should bear me on your shoulders.* The boy clearly is referring to Richard's deformity. Court jesters sometimes carried apes on their shoulders, and travelling showmen often led about with them at country fairs a bear and an ape, the ape on the bear's back. The speech, therefore, as Buckingham points out, is far from complimentary, in whatever sense the reference to the ape is meant. Cf. *Much Ado about Nothing,* II. i. 42-44: 'I will even take sixpence in earnest of the bear-ward, and lead his apes into hell.' See also Autolycus' description of his imaginary robber, *Winter's Tale,* IV. ii. 101.

III. i. 141. The Quarto completes the line by reading 'needs will have it so.'

III. i. 150. S. d. *Sennet.* A set flourish of trumpets, used to mark a royal progress.

III. i. 170. *as it were far off, sound thou Lord Hastings.* '. . . the protector and the duke of Buckingham made verie good semblance vnto the lord Hastings. . . . And vndoubtedlie the protector loued him well, and loth was to haue lost him, sauing for feare least his life should haue quailed their purpose. For which cause he mooued Catesbie to prooue with some words cast out a farre off, whether he could thinke it possible to win the lord Hastings vnto their part.' *Holinshed,* iii. 722. *More,* 45/3.

III. i. 185. *Mistress Shore.* She became the mistress of Lord Hastings after the death of Edward IV.

III. i. 195, 196. *The earldom of Hereford, and all the moveables Whereof the king my brother was possess'd.* '. . . it was agreed that . . . the protector should grant him the quiet possession of the earldome of Hereford, which he claimed as his inheritance. . . . Besides these requests of the duke, the protector, of his owne mind, promised him a great quantitie of the kings treasure, and of his household stuffe.' *Holinshed,* iii. 721. *More,* 42/30.

III. ii. 5. *stroke of four.* Dramatically, the next day after the action of the last scene. Historically, midnight of June 12-13, 1483.

III. ii. 20. *separated council.* 'But the protector and the duke, after that they had sent the lord cardinall, the archbishop of Yorke, then lord chancellor, the bishop of Elie, the lord Stanleie, and the lord Hastings, then lord chamberleine, with manie other noble men, to common & deuise about the coronation in one place, as fast were they in an other place, contriuing the contrarie, and to make the protector king.' *Holinshed,* iii. 721. *More,* 43/6. Hastings' trust in Catesby and the latter's betrayal of the lord is described in *Holinshed,* iii. 722, and *More,* 44/8.

III. ii. 26. *his dreams.* '. . . the selfe night next before his death, the lord Stanleie sent a trustie messenger vnto him [Hastings] at midnight in all the hast, requiring him to rise and ride awaie with him, for he was disposed vtterlie no longer to bide, he had so fearfull a dreame; in which him thought that a boare with his tuskes so rased them both by the heads, that the bloud ran about both their shoulders.' *Holinshed,* iii. 723. *More,* 48/19. Further, in the same passage, Hastings chides the messenger for his master's faith in dreams.

III. ii. 70. *his head upon the bridge.* London Bridge, where the heads of traitors were exposed on a tower.

III. ii. 88. *the day is spent.* The scene opens at four in the morning. The meaning, therefore, is that it is growing late, not that the day is over.

III. ii. 98. *now we meet.* 'Vpon the verie Tower wharfe, so neare the place where his head was off soone after, there met he [the lord Hastings] with one Hastings, a purseuant of his owne name. And, at their meeting in that place, he was put in remembrance of another time, in which it had happened them before to meet in like manner togither in the same place. At which time the lord chamberleine had beene accused vnto king Edward by the lord Riuers, the queenes brother. . . .' See also the rest of the passage. *Holinshed,* iii. 723. *More,* 50/9.

III. ii. 108. *Sir John.* Sir, a title formerly applied to priests and curates in general. The 'sir' has reference to the degree of bachelor of arts, being the usual English equivalent of the Latin *dominus.* Sir John was a common nickname for priests.

III. ii. 112. *talking with a priest.* In Holinshed it is not Buckingham but a knight who is sent by Richard to accompany Hastings to the council. The knight finds Hastings in Tower Street, talking with a priest. ' "What, my lord, I pray you come on, whereto talke you so long with that priest? you haue no need of a priest yet." ' *Holinshed,* iii. 723. *More,* 49/26.

III. ii. 114. *shriving.* Here used equivocally. Its religious meaning includes confessing and doing penance; its legal sense, imposing an obligation or penalty.

III. iii. S. d. The historical date of Rivers' execution could not have been earlier than June 23, 1483, for he made his will on that day. *Excerpta Historica,* 246, ed. 1831. Hastings was executed on June 13. Shakespeare assigns, dramatically, the execution of these two lords to the same day, June 13. In this he follows *Holinshed,* iii. 725, and *More,* 55/25.

III. iii. 11. *Richard the Second here was hack'd to death.* Cf. *Richard II,* V. v. 106-112.

III. iii. 14. *Margaret's curse.* Margaret did not, as a matter of fact, 'exclaim on' Grey, but on Rivers, Dorset, and Hastings. See I. iii. 220-224.

III. iv. 26. *cue.* Words preceding each speech,

learned by an actor when studying his part, to enable him to speak at the proper moment for his lines.

III. iv. 32. *good strawberries.* '[Richard] said vnto the bishop of Elie: "My lord, you haue verie good strawberies at your garden in Holborn, I require you let vs haue a messe of them." "Gladlie, my lord" (quoth he) "would God I had some better thing as readie to your pleasure as that." ' *Holinshed,* iii. 722. *More, 45/24.*

III. iv. 58 S. d. 'And soone . . . he returned into the chamber amongst them, all changed, with a woonderfull soure angrie countenance, knitting the browes, frowning, and fretting and gnawing on his lips . . . thus he began: "What were they worthie to haue that compasse and imagine the destruction of me, being so neere of bloud vnto the king, and protector of his roiall person and his realm? . . . Ye shall all see in what wise that sorceresse [the queene], and that other witch of hir councell, Shores wife, . . . by their sorcerie and witchcraft, wasted my bodie." ' *Holinshed,* iii. 722. *More, 45/24.*

III. iv. 69. *blasted sapling.* Cf. *3 Henry VI*, III. ii. 155, 156: 'She did corrupt frail nature with some bribe, To shrink mine arm up like a wither'd shrub.'

III. iv. 74. *If.* '[Hastings] said: "Certeinlie, my lord, if they haue so heinouslie doone, they be worthie heinous punishment." "What" (quoth the protector) "thou seruest me, I weene, with 'ifs' and with 'ands': I tell thee they haue so doone, and that I will make good on thy bodie, traitor ! . . . for, by saint Paule" (quoth he) "I will not to dinner till I see thy head off !" ' *Holinshed,* iii. 722. *More, 45/24.*

III. iv. 84. *my foot-cloth horse did stumble.* The foot-cloth was a large, richly ornamented cloth laid over the back of a horse, and hanging down to the ground on each side. It was an old belief that the stumbling of a rider's horse was an omen of some great misfortune. 'Certeine is it also, that in riding towards the Tower, the same morning in which he was beheaded, his horsse twise or thrise stumbled with him, almost to the falling.' *Holinshed*, iii. 723. *More*, 49/18.

III. iv. 98. *air of your good looks.* I.e. favorable breeze of your good outward appearance (See 'air,' Murray, N.E.D.).

III. iv. 99. *drunken sailor on a mast.* Cf. *Proverbs*, xxiii, 34: 'Yea, thou shalt be as he . . . that lieth upon the top of a mast.' The figure is repeated in *2 Henry IV*, III. i. 18-25.

III. v. 40. *Turks.* Elizabethan writers often used this term as a synonym for infidel. See *Prayer Book*, third collect for Good Friday: 'Turks, Infidels and Hereticks.'

III. v. 49, 50. The Quarto assigns these two lines to the Mayor.

III. v. 68. *too late of our intent.* I.e. too late to learn in advance of our purpose.

III. v. 75. *a citizen.* For an account of Richard's reference see Boswell-Stone, *Shakespeare's Holinshed*, p. 375, note 2. The story is quoted by Halle and likewise is to be found in Grafton, ii. 107.

III. v. 78. *sign.* Richard means that the citizen's shop was designated by a signboard with a crown painted on it.

III. v. 84. *thus far come near my person.* I.e. thus far make intimate reference to me myself.

III. v. 97. *Baynard's Castle.* On the Thames between Blackfriars and London Bridge. In Shakespeare's time the castle belonged to William Herbert, the Earl of Pembroke.

III. v. 102. *Doctor Shaw.* 'Iohn Shaw, clearke, brother to the maior.' *Holinshed*, iii. 725.

III. v. 103. *Friar Penker.* 'frier Penker, prouinciall of the Augustine Friers.' *Holinshed*, iii. 725.

III. vii. 5. *Lady Lucy*. The pre-contract was said to have been with Elizabeth Lucy, who was one of Edward's mistresses. '[Buckingham tells the citizens how Dr. Shaw] groundlie made open vnto you, the children of King Edward the fourth were neuer lawfullie begotten; forsomuch as the king (leauing his verie wife dame Elizabeth Lucie) was neuer lawfullie maried vnto the queene their mother. . . .' *Holinshed*, iii. 729. *More*, 70/21. Buckingham also declared that 'the king's greedie appetite was insatiable, and euerie where ouer all the realme intollerable.' *Holinshed*, iii. 729. Buckingham likewise makes references to the things spoken of by Doctor Shaw 'as 'twere far off.'

III. vii. 6. *contract by deputy*. See *3 Henry VI*, III. iii. 49 ff. for an account of this. The lady was Bona, daughter of the Duke of Savoy, and sister of the French queen.

III. vii. 15. *victories*. Richard commanded an expedition against Scotland in 1482, advancing as far as Edinburgh. Berwick was captured and ceded to England when peace was concluded.

III. vii. 25. *statues*. 'When the duke had said, and looked that the people, whome he hoped that the maior had framed before, should, after this proposition made, haue cried, "King Richard, king Richard!" all was husht and mute, and not one word answered therevnto. . . .' *Holinshed*, 730. *More*, 72/16. Holinshed further describes Buckingham's efforts in substance as Shakespeare represents in this scene.

III. vii. 44-245. The historical time of the rest of this scene is June 25, 1483, the day after Buckingham's speech at the Guildhall. Shakespeare makes one dramatic day of the whole scene. *More's* order of events places Shaw's sermon on June 15 and Buckingham's speech on June 17. For an account of the Lord Mayor and his reception by Richard, see *Holinshed*,

iii. 731, and *More,* 74/27. There is no historical authority for Richard's refusal of an audience on the ground of preoccupation with 'holy Exercise.'

III. vii. 50. *maid's part.* I.e. with reference to the proverbial saying 'A Woman's nay doth stand for naught.' See *Two Gentlemen of Verona,* I. ii. 53, 54: 'Since maids, in modesty, say "No" to that Which they would have the profferer construe "Ay." '

III. vii. 140-172. Richard's reply is mainly Shakespeare's invention save for lines 148-150 and line 171, which are based on *Holinshed,* iii. 731; *More,* 75/20.

III. vii. 165. *And much I need to help you, were there need.* 'I want much of the ability requisite to give you help, if help were needed' (Johnson); 'And much I ought to help you if you need help' (The Cowden-Clarkes). Dr. Johnson's paraphrase seems the more satisfactory.

III. vii. 171. *happy stars.* A reference to the pseudo-science of astrology, meaning 'favorable conjunction of planets in his horoscope.'

III. vii. 179. *a witness.* '[The Duchess of York] openlie obiected against his mariage, (as it were in discharge of hir conscience,) that the king was sure to dame Elizabeth Lucie and hir husband before God.' *Holinshed,* iii. 727. *More,* 61/31. For the rest of this scene, see *Holinshed,* iii. 731, *More,* 77/11.

III. vii. 187. *pitch.* A technical term from falconry meaning the highest point in the flight of a falcon.

III. vii. 188. *bigamy.* A statute in 4 Edw. I defined one aspect of bigamy as the marrying of a widow. Note that in the play Richard himself is guilty of 'bigamy,' if this definition is followed.

IV. i. 32. *crowned.* The coronation was held in Westminster Abbey on July 6, 1483.

IV. i. 42. *Richmond.* Dorset went with Queen Elizabeth into sanctuary at Westminster (*Polydore*

Vergil, 540), and left it to join the rebellion raised by
Buckingham in October, 1483 (*Holinshed*, iii. 743).
After Buckingham's capture, Dorset succeeded in
escaping by sea and 'arriued safelie in the duchie of
Britaine.' *Holinshed*, iii. 743. *Halle*, 394.

IV. i. 54. *cockatrice*. See note on 'basilisk,' I. ii.
150.

IV. i. 85. *Warwick*. Warwick was killed fighting on
the Lancastrian side in the battle of Barnet, where
Richard was one of the Yorkist generals.

IV. i. 95. *Eighty odd*. The Duchess of York was
born in 1415, and therefore was only sixty-eight in
1483.

IV. ii. 8. *play the touch*. The touchstone was a
black jasper from India used by Italian goldsmiths in
testing the genuineness of gold (King). There are
many references to touchstones in Elizabethan litera-
ture. Cf. *1 Henry IV*, IV. iv. 10: 'To-morrow . . .
is a day Wherein the fortune of ten thousand men
Must bide the touch.'

IV. ii. 40. *His name, my lord, is Tyrrell*. ' "Sir"
(quoth his page) "there lieth one on your pallet without, that I dare well saie, to doo your grace pleasure,
the thing were right hard that he would refuse."
Meaning this by sir Iames Tirrell. . . .' *Holinshed*,
iii. 734. *More*, 81/15. In the same passage Holinshed records that when Richard broached the matter
to Sir James 'he found him nothing strange.'

IV. ii. 51. *grievous sick*. '[Richard] procured a
common rumor (but he would not haue the author
knowne) to be published and spred abroad among the
common people, that the queene was dead; to the intent that she, taking some conceit of this strange
fame, should fall into some sudden sicknesse or
greeuous maladie. . . .' *Holinshed*, iii. 751. *Halle*,
407.

IV. ii. 60. *brother's daughter*. *Stow* gives March

16, 1485, as the date of Anne's death. '[Richard] intended shortlie to marie the ladie Elizabeth, his
brothers daughter.' *Holinshed,* iii. 751. *Halle,* 407.

IV. ii. 91. *wife.* In 1484, according to Holinshed,
there was surprise that the Lord Stanley had not been
arrested as a reputed enemy of Richard, for Margaret,
Stanley's wife, was mother to the Earl of Richmond.
Holinshed, iii. 746. *Halle,* 398.

IV. ii. 95. *prophesy.* This prophecy will be found
in *Holinshed,* iii. 678.

IV. ii. 98-115. This passage occurs only in the
Quarto.

IV. ii. 104. *Rougemont.* Richard visited Exeter in
November, 1483. 'And during his abode here he went
about the citie, & viewed the seat of the same, & at
length he came to the castell; and, when he vnder-
stood that it was called Rugemont, suddenlie he fell
into a dumpe, and (as one astonied) said: "Well, I
see my daies be not long." He spake this of a prophesie
told him, that, when he came once to Richmond, he
should not long liue after. . . .' *Holinshed,* iii. 746.

IV. ii. 113. *Jack.* The figure which in old clocks
struck the hour upon the bell. The word came to be
a nickname for a busybody (Wright). Cf. *Richard
II,* V. v. 60: 'his Jack o' the clock.'

IV. ii. 116. *resolve.* 'And, suerlie, the occasion of
their variance is of diuerse men diuerslie reported.
Some haue I heard say, that the duke [Buckingham],
a little before his [Richard's] coronation, among other
things, required of the protector the erle of Herefords
lands, to the which he pretended himself iust inheritor.
. . . [Richard] reiected the dukes request with manie
spitefull and minatorie words.' *Holinshed,* iii. 736.
More, 86/29.

IV. ii. 121. *Brecknock.* A castle and property in
Wales belonging to the Duke of Buckingham.

IV. iii. 6. *flesh'd.* A term derived from hunting.

Hounds were said to be fleshed when they ate of the first game which they killed. See note on lines 9, 10 below.

IV. iii. 9, 10. *Dighton . . . Forrest.* '. . . sir Iames Tirrell deuised, that they should be murthered in their beds. To the execution whereof, he appointed Miles Forrest, one of the foure that kept them, a fellow fleshed in murther before time. To him he ioined one Iohn Dighton, his owne horssekeeper, a big, broad square, and strong knaue.' *Holinshed,* iii. 735. *More,* 83/23. The qualms of the murderers are Shakespeare's own additions. According to Holinshed, in the same passage, Sir James would not admit to Richard that he knew the princes had been buried in 'so vile a corner' as under 'the stair foot, beneath a heap of stones.' See l. 30.

IV. iii. 36. *pent up.* Edward Plantagenet, Earl of Warwick, son of George Duke of Clarence 'had beene kept in prison within the Tower almost from his tender yeares.' *Holinshed,* iii. 787. *Halle,* 490.

IV. iii. 37. *daughter.* Margaret Plantagenet, Countess of Salisbury, Clarence's daughter, was born August, 1473, and therefore was about twelve years old at Richard's death. Shakespeare has perhaps confused her with her first cousin. It was, according to Holinshed, the Lady Cicely, sister of Elizabeth, Richard's niece, that Richard planned to marry to a man of 'an vnknowne linage and familie.' *Holinshed,* iii. 752. *Halle,* 409.

IV. iii. 38. *Abraham's bosom.* Cf. *St. Luke,* xvi, 22: 'And it came to pass, that the beggar died, and was carried by the angels into Abraham's bosom. . . .'

IV. iii. 40. *Britaine.* Richmond was in exile in Brittany.

IV. iii. 43. S. d. *Ratcliff.* The Quarto reading is 'Catesby,' and this has been generally accepted by subsequent editors.

IV. iii. 46. *Morton.* '. . . sailed into Flanders, where he did the earle of Richmond good seruice.' *Holinshed,* iii. 741. *Halle,* 390.

IV. iii. 48. *power.* The date of the beginning of Buckingham's revolt is October 18, 1483, according to the attainder of Buckingham, *Rotuli Parliamentorum,* vi, 245. For an account of Buckingham's march with his Welshmen, cf. *Holinshed,* iii. 743, *Halle,* 394.

IV. iii. 55. *Jove's Mercury.* Mercury was the messenger who carried the commands of Jove.

IV. iv. 6. *to France.* Actually, Margaret went to France in 1476, after which time she did not again return to England. See note, I. iii. 167.

IV. iv. 15. *right for right.* Justice answering to the claims of justice (Johnson).

IV. iv. 28. *abstract.* Cf. *Hamlet,* II. ii. 555: 'for they are the abstracts and brief chronicles of the time.'

IV. iv. 52, 53. These two lines are reversed in the Quarto, which makes a rather better sequence, though either can be defended. The Folio printer's eye may have been confused by three consecutive lines beginning with 'That.'

IV. iv. 52. *galled eyes.* So too in *Hamlet,* I. ii. 155: 'Ere yet the salt of most unrighteous tears Had left the flushing in her galled eyes. . . .'

IV. iv. 85. *index . . . pageant.* The 'index' was the written prologue sometimes distributed to the audience to explain the allegory in the 'pageant' or dumb-show (pantomimic action) to follow. The reference of course is to the representation of a play with a dumb-show. The 'index' here is said to have promised a happier conclusion than afterwards came to pass (Stevens; Wright).

IV. iv. 88-90. These lines are obviously confused in the arrangement of the Quarto. For the Quarto reading, see list of variants, Appendix C.

IV. iv. 105. Cf. *Love's Labour's Lost*, IV. iii. 384: 'And justice always whirls in equal measure.'

IV. iv. 128. *intestate*. The Folio reading is 'intestine.' There seems little doubt that 'intestine' is either a misprint or an attempted correction arising from a misunderstanding of the manuscript. The reading of the Quarto has, therefore, been adopted in this text.

IV. iv. 148. This line is omitted in the Quarto, and the query concerning Hastings is added to the preceding line of the Queen.

IV. iv. 176. *Humphrey Hour*. No satisfactory explanation of this apparent sarcasm of Richard's has yet been made. Those who lacked the price of a meal were said to dine with Duke Humphrey, but how the saying is meant to be applied here is not clear.

IV. iv. 204. *Elizabeth*. '[Richard] would rather take to wife his cousine and neece the ladie Elizabeth, than for lacke of that affinitie the whole realme should run to ruine. . . . Wherefore he sent to the queene (being in sanctuarie) diuerse and often messengers, which . . . should so largelie promise promotions innumerable, and benefits, not onelie to hir, but also to hir sonne lord Thomas, Marquesse Dorset. . . .' *Holinshed*, 750. *Halle*, 406. The passage further describes how the queen 'began somewhat to relent.'

IV. iv. 216. *opposite*. According to the pseudo-science of astrology the 'opposition' of beneficent stars neutralised their good effects, turning them to evil aspects.

IV. iv. 226. Cf. *Hamlet*, II. i. 66: 'By indirections find directions out.'

IV. iv. 236-239. *so thrive* . . . I.e. May the success of my enterprise be as assured, as are my good intents toward you and yours in the future.

IV. iv. 251. *Lethe*. A river of the Greek under-

world whose waters produced forgetfulness in the
souls who drank of it.

IV. iv. 276. Cf. *3 Henry VI,* I. iv. 79-83, and I.
iii. 178 above.

IV. iv. 284. *conveyance.* Cf. *3 Henry VI,* III.
iii. 160: 'Thy sly conveyance and thy lord's false love.'

IV. iv. 289. Richard repeats the argument he used
to Anne in I. ii. 115-124.

IV. iv. 312. *Dorset.* Shakespeare ignores historical
time here. Dorset first joined with Buckingham. That
expedition failed in October, 1483. He then went
abroad and joined Richmond, who set out on his suc-
cessful expedition in August, 1485. (See, also, IV. i.
41, 42, and IV. ii. 48, 49 above.)

IV. iv. 324. *love.* Theobald's emendation 'loan'
has been generally accepted by modern editors.

IV. iv. 333. Cf. Richard's earlier references: 'The
deep-revolving, witty Buckingham,' IV. ii. 42; 'High-
reaching Buckingham,' IV. ii. 31.

IV. iv. 347. *king's King forbids.* The reference is
to marriage within forbidden degrees of kinship. Cf.
Leviticus, xviii, 14: 'Thou shalt not uncover the naked-
ness of thy father's brother, thou shalt not approach
to his wife. . . .'

IV. iv. 365, 366. The Folio transposes these two
lines. 366 is omitted in the Quartos from 2 through
8. It is probable, therefore, that in editing the Folio
text an error occurred in the insertion of the missing
line. The expression to 'harp on a string' was a common one.

IV. iv. 367. *George.* An anachronism. The image
of St. George on horseback, tilting at the dragon,
was added to the collar of the badge of the Garter by
Henry VIII (Ashmole).

IV. iv. 375. In the Quarto this line follows 'thy
life hath it dishonour'd.'

IV. iv. 378. *God.* As elsewhere in the Folio text,

the oaths have been modified to conform to the statute against blasphemy. The Folio here substitutes 'Heaven' for 'God.'

IV. iv. 381. *brothers*. Earl Rivers is the only brother of Elizabeth introduced in the present play.

IV. iv. 397. The Folio here reads 'repast.' Editors are agreed in regarding this as a misprint for the 'o'erpast' of the Quarto.

IV. iv. 401. This line is omitted in the Quarto.

IV. iv. 418. *found*. Many editors adopt the Quarto reading 'peevish-fond.'

IV. iv. 425. Steevens notes here a reference to the fable of the phoenix.

IV. iv. 439. *hull*. Literally, to float or be driven by the force of the wind or current on the hull alone; to drift to the wind with sails furled; to lie a-hull (Murray, N.E.D.).

IV. iv. 441. *Norfolk*. On hearing of Richmond's landing, Richard 'sent to Iohn duke of Norffolke, . . . and to other of his especiall & trustie friends of the nobilitie, . . . willing them to muster and view all their seruants and tenants, . . . and with them to repaire to his presence with all speed and diligence.' *Holinshed,* iii. 754. *Halle,* 412.

IV. iv. 445. *Ratcliff*. The Folio reading 'Catesby' (for Ratcliff) here is regarded by editors either as a misprint or an oversight.

Salisbury. Richmond was off the southwestern coast, close to Dorset. At Salisbury Richard would be able to prevent a junction with Buckingham's forces coming from Wales. '[Richard] tooke his iournie toward Salisburie, to the intent that in his iournie he might set on the dukes [Buckingham's] armie. . . .' *Holinshed,* iii. 743. *Halle,* 394.

IV. iv. 477. *Welshman*. On his father's side. Richmond's father was the son of Owen Tudor and Katherine, widow of Henry V.

IV. iv. 479. '[Richard] most mistrusted . . . Thomas lord Stanleie . . . For when the said lord Stanleie would haue departed into his countrie . . . the king in no wise would suffer him to depart, before he had left as an hostage in the court George Stanleie, lord Strange, his first begotten sonne and heire.' *Holinshed,* iii. 751. *Halle,* 408.

IV. iv. 501. *Sir Edward Courtney.* Sir Edward Courtenay of Haccombe. He was created Earl of Devon on Henry VII's accession. For an account of these risings, see *Holinshed,* iii. 743. *Halle,* 393.

IV. iv. 502. *Bishop of Exeter.* Shakespeare followed More's error in calling Peter Courtenay, Bishop of Exeter, brother of Sir Edward. Peter was the son of Sir Philip Courtenay of Powderham. The Bishop was the cousin of Sir Edward.

IV. iv. 504. *the Guildfords.* The Guildfords were a distinguished family seated at Hempstead, near Cranbrook, Kent.

IV. iv. 508. *owls! nothing but songs of death.* According to Pliny the cry of the screech-owl always betokened 'some heavy news.'

IV. iv. 513. 'By this floud the passages were so closed, that neither the duke could come ouer Severn to his adherents or they to him. . . . The duke (being thus left almost post alone) was of necessitie compelled to flie. . . .' *Holinshed,* iii. 743. *Halle,* 394. On October 23, 1483, Richard 'made proclamation, that what person could shew and reueale where the duke of Buckingham was, should be highlie rewarded. . . .' *Holinshed,* iii. 744. *Halle,* 394.

IV. iv. 522. *tempest.* Richmond sailed Oct. 12, 1483, and the same night the great storm arose that dispersed his fleet. The first ill-fated expedition is described in *Holinshed,* iii. 744. *Halle,* 396.

IV. iv. 532. Buckingham was taken at Shrewsbury in October, 1483.

IV. iv. 534. *landed.* Richmond, on his second expedition, landed at Milford Haven in August, 1485. Shakespeare has condensed, therefore, the history of two years in this scene.

IV. v. 4. *If I revolt.* 'For the lord Stanleie was afraid, least, if he should seeme openlie to be a fautor or aider to the earle his sonne in law, before the day of the battell, that king Richard, (which yet vtterlie did not put him in diffidence and mistrust,) would put to some cruell death his sonne and heire apparant. . . .' *Holinshed,* iii. 753. *Halle,* 411.

IV. v. 12-15. Sir Walter Herbert, created by Edward IV Baron Herbert; Sir Gilbert Talbot, uncle to the young Earl of Shrewsbury; Sir William Stanley, the brother of Richmond's step-father; redoubted Pembroke, Jasper Tudor, Richmond's uncle; Oxford and Sir James Blunt had come from France with Richmond; Rhys ap Thomas, a valiant Welsh leader from Carmarthenshire.

V. i. 10. *All-Souls' day.* '[Buckingham] vpon All soules daie, without arreignment or iudgement . . . was at Salisburie, in the open market place, on a new scaffold, beheaded and put to death.' *Holinshed,* iii. 744. *Halle,* 395.

V. i. 13. Cf. II. i. 32-40.

V. i. 19. *determin'd . . . wrongs.* I.e. the fixed period to which the punishment of my wrong-doing is postponed (Wright).

V. i. 25. Cf. I. iii. 299-303.

V. ii. 8. Cf. *Psalm* lxxx: 'The wild boar out of the field doth root it [the vine] up: and the wild beasts of the field devour it.'

V. ii. 20. *friends for fear.* 'Diuerse other noble personages, which inwardlie hated king Richard woorse than a tode or a serpent, did likewise resort to him with all their power and strength, wishing and working his destruction. . . .' *Holinshed,* iii. 745. *Halle,* 413.

V. iii. S. d. *Earl of Surrey.* This character is omitted in the quartos.

V. iii. 11. *battalia.* '[Richmond's] whole number exceeded not fiue thousand men, beside the power of the Stanleies, wherof three thousand were in the field. . . .' *Holinshed,* iii. 755. *Halle,* 414.

V. iii. 12. *tower.* Cf. *Proverbs,* xviii, 10: 'The name of the Lord is a strong tower.'

V. iii. 18 S. d. *Dorset.* He was not at Bosworth Field, having been left behind in France by Richmond.

V. iii. 63. *watch.* It is possible that 'watch' means here, as Doctor Johnson suggested, a watch-light or candle.

V. iii. 96. *tender George.* Shakespeare seems to have been unaware that George Stanley was at this time a grown man. 'The child' of the chronicles is the same use of the word as in the ballad quoted in *King Lear,* III. iv. 187, meaning 'young nobleman.'

V. iii. 111. *bruising irons of wrath.* Cf. *Psalm* ii, 9: 'Thou shalt bruise them with a rod of iron.'

V. iii. 119. *Richard's dream.* 'The fame went, that he had the same night a dreadfull and terrible dreame: for it seemed to him being asleepe, that he did see diuerse images like terrible diuels, which pulled and haled him, not suffering him to take anie quiet or rest. . . .' *Holinshed,* iii. 755. *Halle,* 414.

V. iii. 144. *lance.* Some editors emend this line by the insertion of an adjective such as Collier's 'point-less' before 'lance.' As any such emendation rests upon no valid authority, the line should remain as it stands in the text.

V. iii. 153. *laid.* Many editors prefer the reading 'lead' of the first Quarto. In all the Folios, however, and in the quartos from 2 through 8 the reading is 'laid' or 'layd.'

V. iii. 174. *for hope.* Wright's paraphrase 'I died as regards hope' is probably correct, since it is confirmed by a passage in Greene's *James IV,* V. vi. (Dyce ed., p. 217). Steevens suggested 'I died for hoping to give you aid, before I could actually give it.'

V. iii. 180. *coward conscience.* Cf. *Hamlet,* III. i. 83: 'Thus conscience does make cowards of us all.'

V. iii. 181. *lights burn blue.* There was an old superstition to the effect that spirits signified their presence by causing lights to become dim or to burn blue. Cf. *Julius Cæsar,* IV. iii. 274: (at entrance of Ghost of Cæsar) 'How ill this taper burns!'

now. The 'not' of the Folio is probably a misprint. Cf. *Hamlet,* III. ii. 413: ' 'Tis now the very witching time of night, When churchyards yawn, and hell itself breathes out Contagion to this world.'

V. iii. 183. The punctuation of the line in the Quarto deserves consideration: 'What do I feare? my selfe?'

V. iii. 202. *shall.* The Quarto reading 'will' has been generally accepted.

V. iii. 213-215. These lines are omitted in the Folio, by 'an accident of the press,' according to Spedding.

V. iii. 222. *eaves-dropper.* The Folio 'ease-drop-per' appears to be a misprint, although the same reading occurs in the quartos. The fourth Folio is the first text to make the emendation 'eaves-dropper.'

V. iii. 232. *cried on.* An idiomatic expression. Cf. *Hamlet,* V. ii. 378: 'This quarry cries on havoc';

Othello, V. i. 47: 'whose noise is this that cries on murther?'

V. iii. 238. For the substance of this oration, see *Holinshed,* iii. 757, 758. *Halle,* 417.

V. iii. 256. *swear.* The Quarto 'sweat' is probably correct.

V. iii. 305. *Jockey.* This couplet is in *Holinshed,* iii. 759, with the difference of 'Iacke' for 'Jockey.'

V. iii. 315. For the substance of Richard's oration, see *Holinshed,* iii. 756, and *Halle,* 415.

V. iii. 345. 'When king Richard was come to Bosworth, he sent a purseuant to the lord Stanleie, commanding him to aduance forward with his companie, and to come to his presence; which thing if he refused to doo, he sware, by Christes passion that he would strike off his sonnes head before he dined.' *Holinshed,* iii. 760. Halle, 420.

V. iii. 346. *marsh.* 'Betweene both armies there was a great marish then . . . which the earle of Richmond left on his right hand; for this intent, that it should be on that side a defense for his part, and in so dooing he had the sunne at his backe, and in the faces of his enimies. When king Richard saw the earles companie was passed the marish, he did command with all hast to set vpon them.' *Holinshed,* iii. 758. *Halle,* 418.

V. iv. 7. This line was imitated and parodied by several of Shakespeare's contemporaries. See Appendix B.

V. iv. 11. *six Richmonds.* It was not uncommon for a leader to have several of his knights dress like him. Cf. *1 Henry IV,* V. iii. 1-28.

V. iv. 17. *royalty.* The word is in the plural in the Folio.

V. iv. 27. *Brandon.* Sir William Brandon was not slain at Bosworth.

V. iv. 38, 39. Cf. *3 Henry VI*, II. v. Among the characters introduced are 'a Son that hath killed his Father' and 'a Father that hath killed his Son.'

V. iv. 45. *their*. The reading of the Quarto. Folio, 'they.'

APPENDIX A

SOURCES OF THE PLAY

The second edition of Holinshed's *Chronicles* (1st ed., 1577; 2d ed., 1587) is the chief historical source of *Richard III*. Often the account in Holinshed is a paraphrase of Halle, *The Vnion of the two noble and illustre famelies of Lancastre and Yorke* (1550),[1] which in turn is based upon Sir Thomas More's *History of King Richard the thirde*, published 1513. The authorship of More's history has been attributed to Cardinal Morton, who died in 1500. For matter not in More, Halle was indebted to Polydore Vergil's *Historia Angliæ*, Basel, 1555. Textual references to Holinshed, Halle, and More in this edition are derived from *Shakspere's Holinshed*, edited by W. G. Boswell-Stone, London, 1896. Boswell-Stone's references to More's history are from the text of More's *Workes*, edition of 1557, the paging from J. R. Lumby's edition, 1883.

Matter relating to *Richard III* in the second edition of Holinshed, that is not to be found in the first, is as follows: *Holinshed*, iii. 702 (the fire-new stamp of Dorset's title, I. iii. 255, 256); *Holinshed*, iii. 754 (Richard's friends resorting to him through fear, but wishing and working his destruction, V. ii. 20, 21); *Holinshed*, iii. 757 (Richmond's oration to his army, V. iii. 236); *Holinshed*, iii. 756 (Richard's oration to his army, V. iii. 313); *Holinshed*, iii. 756 (Richmond kept in Brittany by Richard's mother's means, V. iii. 325).

Two plays on Richard's life preceded the first publication of Shakespeare's in 1597. These were Dr. Thomas Legge's *Richardus Tertius*, a tragedy in Latin

---

[1] Page references in the notes are to the edition of 1809.

performed at St. John's College, Cambridge, in 1579, and *The True Tragedie of Richard III, with the conjunction and joining of the two noble houses, Lancaster and Yorke; as it was playd by the Queenes Maiesties Players. 1594.*

Shakespeare owes little or nothing to Dr. Legge's play.[1] There has been considerable difference of opinion concerning the relation of Shakespeare's play to the *True Tragedie.* In general, it is safe to say that there are certain resemblances, such as Richard's cry for "A horse, a horse, a fresh horse," but that Shakespeare's indebtedness hardly extends beyond a few hints. Artistically and dramatically the two plays are from pole to pole apart.[2]

To sum up, Shakespeare's conception of Richard's character consistently follows More; for his incidents, the dramatist used the second edition of Holinshed, inspired perhaps in his choice of subject by the success of the *True Tragedie.* The passages from Holinshed quoted in the notes will illustrate Shakespeare's use of his principal source.

[1] For a full discussion of this point, see G. B. Churchill, *Richard III up to Shakespeare*, pp. 265-395.

[2] Cf. Churchill, *op. cit.,* p. 398. The text of the *True Tragedie* will be found in Furness' *Variorum*, pp. 505-548.

APPENDIX B

THE HISTORY OF THE PLAY

The date of composition of the play, from internal critical evidence, is about the year 1593. The first Quarto appeared in 1597, and editions were frequent thereafter.

The popularity of *Richard III* on the Elizabethan stage appears to have been great, judging from the number of contemporary references and the frequent parodies of the line "A horse! a horse! My kingdom for a horse!"[1] Richard Burbage (c. 1567-1619) probably was the creator of the rôle; in any event there are important contemporary references to his interpretation of Richard. In the *Return from Parnassus* (1601), Pt. 2, IV. iii. Burbage is portrayed as examining a Cambridge student in the art of acting, making him declaim the opening soliloquy of *Richard III.* Manningham's *Diary* for March 13, 1602, refers to an anecdote "vpon a tyme when Burbidge played Richard III." Bishop Corbet's *Iter Boreale* (written before 1635) particularly notes the fame of Burbage's Richard:

"For when he would have sayd 'King Richard dyed,'
  And call'd—'A horse! a horse!'—he Burbidge
      cry'de."

In 1619 a *Funeral Elegy* on Burbage came out, a poem extant in more than one version, containing a reference to his Richard.

---

[1] Peele, *The Battle of Alcazar* (1594); Marston, *Scourge of Villainie* (1598); Heywood, *Edward the Fourth* (pub. 1600); Chapman, *Eastward Hoe* (1605); Marston, *Parasitaster, or the Fawne* (1606), *What You Will* (1607); Heywood, *Iron Age* (1611); Brathwaite, *Strappado for the Divell* (1615); Fletcher and Massinger, *Little French Lawyer* (c. 1620).

"And Crookback, as befits, shall cease to live."

Other contemporary references may be found in J. Munro, *The Shakespeare Allusion Book,* 1909. On the other hand, we possess today no account of an Elizabethan performance of this tragedy, and but one dated reference to a performance before the closing of the theatres in 1642. In Sir Henry Herbert's *Office Book* for the year 1633 there is a note to the effect that *Richard III* was played at St. James' on November 17, before Charles I and Henrietta Maria. In a prologue prefixed to the 1641 edition of Chapman's *Bussy D'Ambois,* one of the actors is recommended because "as Richard he was liked."

When the theatres were reopened after the Restoration, although many of Shakespeare's plays (freely revised or adapted, it is true) were played, there is no record of *Richard III.* The character of Richard, however, continued to appear in plays by other dramatists, notably in John Crowne's *Henry the Sixth, The Second Part, or The Misery of Civil War* (1681), and John Caryl's *The English Princess, or The Death of Richard the Third* (1667). Thomas Betterton (c. 1635-1710), the famous actor of this period, played the Richard of *The English Princess.* Samuel Pepys saw this play on March 7, 1667: "a most sad, melancholy play, and pretty good; but nothing eminent in it, as some tragedys are." In Crowne's drama Betterton played the Earl of Warwick.

On July 9, 1700, Colley Cibber's famous revision of *Richard III* was produced at Drury Lane, a version of the tragedy destined to hold the stage until today.[1] Cibber (1671-1757) himself played Richard in his own version at various revivals up until 1733, and once thereafter (1739). There is not space here to include an analysis of Cibber's version; the text of it may be

[1] Robert Mantell, the contemporary actor, has recently used the Cibber version.

found in Oxberry's collected *British Drama*. In Furness' *Variorum* edition of *Richard III*, page 604, will be found a table of the number of lines retained by Cibber, his borrowings from other Shakespearean plays, and his own additions, all of which totalled some thousand odd lines.[1]

The following revivals of *Richard III*, previous to Garrick's London début are recorded by Genest: Dec. 6, 1715, Drury Lane; March 11, 1721, Lincoln's Inn Fields, with Ryan as Richard. The latter continued to play the part until 1740, challenging rivalry with Cibber of the Drury Lane company in the rôle. In 1732 Ryan and the Lincoln's Inn company moved to Covent Garden. Drury Lane revived the play in 1734 and 1739 with Quin as Richard.

On October 19, 1741, at Goodman's Fields, David Garrick (1717-1779) appeared for the first time on the London stage, choosing for his début the character of Richard the Third. Possibly no first night in the history of the English stage has created a greater sensation than this of Garrick's. It was a triumph, establishing him at once as the foremost actor of the day, a position he retained throughout his life. The secret of Garrick's success, apart from the genius with which he was endowed, was the naturalness of his acting. The playing of tragic rôles had become conventionalized into declamation, rant, artificial gestures and poses. For these defects Garrick substituted an "easy and familiar, yet forcible style in speaking and acting."[2] Garrick played Richard seventeen times that season, and fourteen times the next season at Drury Lane. He continued to play the part at intervals throughout his whole career, his last appearance as Richard being on June 5, 1776, the occasion of his re-

[1] For the classic condemnation of Cibber's version, see Hazlitt, *The Characters of Shakespear's Plays*, essay on *Richard III*.

[2] Davies: *Memoirs of the Life of David Garrick*. 1780.

tirement from the stage. During this year Mrs. Siddons, the great tragic actress, played Lady Anne twice to Garrick's Richard.

Throughout the whole of this time the tragedy (in Cibber's version) remained a public and professional favorite. Many other well-known actors, besides Garrick, appeared as Richard, among them Quin (famous also as a Falstaff), Ryan, Spranger Barry, Mossop, and Thomas Sheridan. In 1746 Garrick challenged Quin to an alternating duel in the character, Quin appearing one night as a representative of the old flamboyant school of tragedy, and Garrick the next to uphold the naturalistic school. The public verdict was overwhelmingly for Garrick. Charles Macklin (1699-1797), an actor of considerable fame and actual merit before the vogue of Garrick, played Richard four times at the age of eighty-five.

In 1789 John Philip Kemble (1757-1823) first appeared in the character of Richard. Kemble was not a believer in naturalistic acting and returned to the school of "high-erected deportment, expressive action, solemn cadence, (and) stately pauses." Kemble's dignity, however, was free from the faults of the ranting pre-Garrick period. "The declamation of Mr. Kemble seemed to be fetched from the schools of philosophy—it was always pure and correct."[1] Kemble played Richard at Drury Lane at intervals until 1802, and at Covent Garden until he left the stage in 1817. Mrs. Siddons usually played Queen Elizabeth to her brother's Richard, and another brother, Charles, played Richmond at the revival of 1811. The next year Charles played Richard.

George Frederick Cooke (1756-1812) after playing Richard several times in the provinces, appeared,

[1] James Boaden: *Memoirs of the Life of John Philip Kemble.* 1825. See also Leigh Hunt: *Critical Essays on the Performers of the London Theatres,* 1807, for an analysis of Kemble's acting.

October 31, 1800, at Covent Garden in the character. When Kemble played in the company with Cooke, the rôle of Richmond was assigned to Kemble. Cooke was the first actor of prominence to play Richard in America. He chose for his début on the American stage the tragedy of *Richard III,* opening in New York on Nov. 21, 1810. He was greatly admired in America, although Lamb has described his Richard as a "butcher-like representation."

In 1805 the "infant Roscius," William Betty, then fourteen years of age and described by his contemporaries as "the tenth wonder of the world," played Richard. Lord Byron had an unfavorable opinion of Master Betty, which he expressed in *English Bards and Scotch Reviewers.*

To Kemble we owe the inauguration of elaborate scenery and the first attempts at accuracy in historical costume in *Richard III,* but the version of Cibber continued to be the text, although Kemble shortened somewhat the Cibber play.

Edmund Kean (1787-1833) attained the greatest fame of any actor of the nineteenth century in Richard. He played it for the first time in London at Drury Lane in 1814, his conception of the character modelled upon the interpretation of George Frederick Cooke, but in reality Kean was so unlike Cooke physically, being small and energetic, that there was little resemblance between the two interpretations. Lord Byron was one of Kean's enthusiastic admirers, as was the poet Keats. It was of Kean's Richard that Coleridge said it was like "reading Shakespeare by flashes of lightning." Kean was a continuer of the Garrick, instead of the Kemble, tradition, to which he added his own peculiar fire and vivacity. As J. P. Kemble pointed out, if one liked the style of Kean, one would not like the style of Kemble. There is, however, no question of the greater popularity of the style of

Kean.[1] The contemporary newspapers are extravagant in their praises: "one of the finest pieces of acting we have ever beheld, or perhaps that the stage has ever known"; and "as the curtain fell the audience rose as one man, cheered lustily, applauded wildly, declaring by word and action this new actor was great indeed." Kean twice played Richard in America in 1820 and 1825. Much of the "traditional" stage-business followed today was originated by Kean.

Kean had but one rival in the part for several years, Junius Brutus Booth (1796-1852) at Covent Garden. He first appeared as Richard Feb. 12, 1817, and although he had his followers, his fame has been eclipsed by the popular glory of his great rival.

The next important Richard was William Charles Macready (1793-1873) who produced the tragedy in London at Covent Garden in 1819, to great applause, thus challenging the supremacy of Kean. Drury Lane responded to the challenge and the two Richards appeared nightly at the rival houses. Genest says of Macready, referring to the revival May 23, 1823: "He was very inferior to Kean, till the ghosts appeared . . . he was then superior." Leigh Hunt said: "Mr. Kean's Richard is the more sombre and perhaps deeper part of him; Mr. Macready's the livelier and more animal part—a very considerable one nevertheless."

On March 12, 1821, Macready attempted the practical restoration of Shakespeare's text, leaving in, however, some of Cibber's lines that had become identified in the popular mind with *Richard III*.[2] But this partial restoration did not find favor and was abandoned after the second performance of it. In his

[1] The best description of the acting of Kean is to be found in W. Hazlitt: *The Characters of Shakespear's Plays*, essay on *Richard III*.

[2] *Reminiscences*, 162. Ed. by Sir Frederick Pollock. 1875.

later revivals in 1831, 1836-7, Macready returned to the Cibber text.

On February 20, 1845, Samuel Phelps (1804-1878) produced *Richard III* at Sadler's Wells, where it ran for about four weeks. Great attention was paid by Phelps to scenery and historical detail. The text used was Shakespeare's with, however, certain cuts. Once more, nevertheless, upon the revival of the tragedy in the season of 1862-3, Phelps returned to the Cibber version.

Perhaps the most elaborate production of *Richard III* yet given was that by Charles Kean (1811-1868) at the Princess Theatre on February 20, 1850. The playbill lists one hundred and twenty-one performers and a formidable array of "authorities" on historical details. All this parade of scholarship did not prevent Charles Kean from using the Cibber version, for which decision he argues at length upon the playbill. Barry Sullivan (1821-1891), in a modified Cibber version, was perhaps the most conspicuous of the lesser actors of the period from Charles Kean to Sir Henry Irving.

Henry Irving (1838-1905) restored Shakespeare's text at the Lyceum on January 29, 1877, with later revivals December 19, 1896, and February 27, 1897. Irving made only the cuts necessary to render the tragedy one of a length suitable for the modern stage, ending with Richard's fall and his second utterance of "a horse a horse, my kingdom for a horse!" Tennyson particularly admired Irving's "Plantagenet look." His interpretation was primarily intellectual.

But two English successors of Irving remain to mention, Sir Herbert Tree (1853-1917) and Sir Francis Robert Benson (1858-). Tree's production was noted for its gorgeous pageantry and the emphasis upon the melodramatic note in Richard; Benson's for its general adequacy. Both followed the text of

Shakespeare. Finally a word must be said, before turning to the history of the play in America, of the Shakespearean productions at the Old Vic, where an excellent stock company has performed all of Shakespeare's plays.

The first recorded performance of a Shakespearean play in America is that of *Richard III*, Cibber version, March 5, 1750, at the theatre in Nassau Street, New York. The Richard was an American, Thomas Kean. The play was repeated the next season. Robert Upton is the second interpreter of Richard in America, January 23, 1752. There is a record of *Richard III* played by an American company in Annapolis in 1752.

In the same year an English company was brought over by Lewis Hallam, with the financial assistance of his brother William. After playing in the Southern Colonies, this English company played *Richard III* on November 12, 1753, at New York. The Richard was a Mr. Rigby, about whose interpretation theatrical history is silent. Another performance of the tragedy was given by Hallam's company on February 7, 1759.

At Philadelphia *Richard III* was performed at the Southwark Theatre in 1766, and on December 14, 1767, one week after the opening of the new John Street theatre at New York the tragedy was performed. Richard trod the boards several times more before the Congress, on October 24, 1778, recommended the suspension of all amusements. The majority of these performances were given by Lewis Hallam.

Major Williams, of the British army of occupation, played Richard at New York in 1779. The tragedy continued, after the Revolution, to be one of the most popular of Shakespeare's plays, the most noteworthy of these earlier players being John Hodgkinson, at New York (1793-4) and James Fennel, at Philadel-

phia's Chestnut Theatre (April 21, 1795). A company
at Boston and strolling companies elsewhere in New
England likewise included *Richard III* in the reper-
tory. Thomas A. Cooper (1776-1849) completes the
list of players of this rôle at the close of the eighteenth
century.

The arrival of George Frederick Cooke at New
York in 1810 began a new era on the American stage.
His Richard was closely imitated by the American
actor, John Duff (1787-1831). Between the two
visits of Edmund Kean to America (1820 and 1825),
came Junius Brutus Booth, who made his first appearance in the part of Richard at the New Park
Theatre on October 5, 1821. Junius Booth continued
to play Richard for the thirty subsequent years of
his career.

Edwin Forrest (1806-1872), the first American
born actor of importance, appeared as Richard at the
Bowery Theatre, New York, on January 23, 1827.
Forrest played Richard as a noble prince, maintaining
that a man of Richard's intellectual power would have
the skill to conceal his deformity. He published a
slightly altered form of Cibber's text.

Before and after the visit of Charles Kean in 1836
and again in 1840, the tragedy underwent some
strange vicissitudes upon our stage. Several "child-
actors" appeared as Richard, among whom were boys
and girls of eleven and less. Ellen Bateman, for
example, played Richard at the age of four. More
than one woman likewise essayed the character. Char-
lotte Crampton gave a performance of the tragedy,
in which, during the last act, she exhibited a troup of
trained horses, thus repeating what had already been
done at the London Astley's where *Richard III* was
once turned into a spectacular circus. Other actors
were fond of using the character of Richard for dis-
playing their powers of mimicry of legitimate players.

It was Edwin Booth (1833-1893) who brought back to our stage the dignity appropriate to this tragedy. As early as 1852 he had made his début as a player in the character of Richard at San Francisco, and appeared for the first time at New York on May 4, 1857. Booth used the Cibber version until 1878, when the distinguished dramatic critic, William Winter, prepared for Booth a version based upon a re-arrangement and cutting of Shakespeare's text.

There is not space to consider all the Richards seen in America. A mere enumeration of such names as the Wallacks, John Edward McCullough, Laurence Barrett, Robert Bruce Mantell, and Richard Mansfield will give some hint of the extensive history of this play upon our stage. But in conclusion a word must be said for the production by Arthur Hopkins of John Barrymore as Richard at New York on March 6, 1920. This was perhaps the best opportunity the present generation has had to judge of the acting merits of this tragedy.[1]

---

[1] For a full account of this play, see *The Stage History of Shakespeare's King Richard the Third,* by Alice I. Perry Wood, Columbia University Press, New York, 1909. The present editor has drawn some of his information from this complete study.

APPENDIX C

The Text of the Present Edition

The text of the present volume is based, by permission of the Oxford University Press, upon that of the Oxford Shakespeare, edited by the late W. J. Craig. Craig's text has been carefully collated with the Quarto of 1597, and with the first Folio of 1623.[1] The textual difficulties in *Richard III* are numerous. The variations between the Quarto of 1597 and the Folio text are striking. Craig inclined to lean upon the authority of the Quarto; the present editor has relied mainly upon the Folio, since the trend of recent editors has been toward a return to this text.

The Folio contains nearly two hundred lines not found in the Quarto, together with many minor changes of words and additions of several short lines and parts of lines. The longer passages of the Folio are not questioned, even by advocates of the Quarto text, as un-Shakespearean. Further, the stage directions of the Folio are more complete and detailed. Apart, therefore, from obvious errors of the press to be found in the Folio, its major variations are admittedly of Shakespearean origin.

There are, however, in the Quarto some lines which do not occur in the Folio, though they are considerably less in number than the additions of the later text. In the second scene of the fourth act, for example, there is a passage, found only in the Quarto, which is dramatically essential. All such lines and passages belonging exclusively to the Quarto have been included within square brackets. Difficulties resulting from ob-

[1] In all, six quartos appeared before the publication of the First Folio, in the following years: 1597, 1598, 1602, 1605, 1612, 1622.

vious errors of the press in the Folio text have been mentioned in the notes.[1]

The following deviations from Craig's text have been introduced:

1. The stage directions of the Folio have been restored. Necessary words and directions, omitted by the Folio, are added within square brackets.

2. Passages occurring in the Quarto but not in the Folio have been placed within square brackets.

3. Spelling has been normalized to accord with modern English practice: e.g. 'villainy.' The punctuation also has been standardized.

4. A few words such as 'murther,' 'burthen,' 'Britaine,' have been left in their original form.

5. The following changes of text have been introduced, usually in accordance with Folio authority. The readings of the present edition precede the colon, while Craig's readings follow it.

I. i. 52 but F: for
65 tempts him to this harsh extremity F: tempers him to this extremity
75 was for delivery? F: was to her for his delivery?
88 and F: an
103 do beseech F: beseech
133 play F: prey
138 John F: Paul
that F: this
142 Where is he, F: What, is he
ii. 19 wolves, to F: adders
31 this F: the
39 stand'st F: stand
76 crimes F: evils
78 of F: of a

[1] For a discussion of the textual problems see: J. Spedding, *On the Quarto and Folio of Richard III,* Shakespeare Society Transactions, 1875-1876, pp. 1-75 and p. 189; E. H. Pickersgill, *On the Quarto and Folio of Richard III,* op. cit., 1875-1876, p. 79 ff.; The Cambridge edition, by W. G. Clark and W. A. Wright; P. A. Daniel, *Preface to Griggs' Facsimile of the Quarto of 1597,* 1884.

79	Of F: For
86	shalt F: shoulds't
88	That F: Which
106	better F: fitter
108	holp F: help'd
117	something F: somewhat
125	I might F: might I
127	rent F: rend
178	naked F: open
213	house F: place
235	my F: her
237	I no friends F: nothing I
243	Tewkesbury F: Tewsbury
252	halts F: halt
iii. 12	unto F: into
41	height F: highest
43	is it . . . complains F: are they . . . complain
47	look F: speak
58	grace F: person
68	thereby he may learn F: that thereby he may gather
77	I F: we
97	desert F: deserts
101	bachelor, and F: bachelor
115	avouch 't F: avouch
118	do remember F: remember
125	spent F: spilt
132	this F: now
147	sov'reign F: lawful
155	A F: As
200	our F: my
	that F: which
204	death F: lose
231	heavy mother's F: mother's heavy
304	an F: on
321	yours, my gracious F: you my noble
333	Dorset F: Vaughan
336	villainy F: villany
iv. 3	fearful dream, of ugly sights F: ugly sights, of ghastly dreams
9	Methoughts F: Methought
13	there F: thence
21	O Lord, F: Lord, Lord!
35	these F: those
41	Who F: Which
46	sour F: grim

50	spake F: cried
52	wand'ring F: wandering
57	him, Furies: F: him! Furies,
66	Ah, Keeper, Keeper! F: O Brakenbury
73	Keeper, I prythee sit by me a while; F: I pray thee, gentle keeper, stay by me;
82	naine F: names
86	*Second* F: *First*
89	*First* F: *Sec.*
94	from F: of
96	king, F: king
104-105	Why, he shall never wake until the great judgment day. F: When he wakes! why, fool, he shall never wake till the judgment day.
112	warrant, F: warrant for it;
121	this passionate humour of mine F: my holy humour
129	Come, F: 'Zounds!
132	Oh, in F: In
133	When F: So when
142	shamefac'd F: shamefast
144	a man F: one
145	that, by chance, F: that
146	of F: of all
150	'Tis F: 'Zounds! It is
155	I F: Tut, I
157	thy F: his
158	fall to work? F: to this gear?
160	on F: over
163	and make F: make
170	*Sec.* F: *First*
181	*Sec.* F: *Both*
190	drawn F: call'd
	among F: from out
198	for any goodness F: to have redemption
204	vassals F: vassal
233	faults F: fault
243	*First* F: *Both*
252	Come, you deceive yourself F: Thou deceiv'st thyself
260	Have you F: Hast thou
	your F: thy
	souls F: soul
263	are you F: art thou
	your F: thy
	souls F: soul

	you will F: thou wilt
264	they F: he
II. i. 5	to F: in
18	is F: are
	from F: in
39	heaven F: God
45	Sir Richard Ratcliff and the duke F: the noble duke
56	unwillingly F: unwittingly
58	To F: By
66	Of you, and you, Lord Rivers, and of Dorset F: Of you, Lord Rivers, and Lord Grey, of you
ii. 8	both F: much
12	Then you conclude, my grandam F: Then, grandam, you conclude
26	a F: his
28	visor F: vizard
41	when the root is gone F: now the root is wither'd
46	ne'er-changing night F: perpetual rest
58	hands F: limbs
60	moan F: grief
61	woes F: plaints
103	help our F: cure their
107	breast F: mind
117	hates F: hearts
121	fet F: fetch'd
143	sister F: mother
iii. 13	Which F: That
43	Pursuing F: Ensuing
iv. 9	good F: young
53	blood F: death
65	earth F: death
III. i. 87	his F: this
91	And F: An
96	noble F: loving
97	dear F: dread
123	as, as F: as
141	will F: needs will
143	should F: would
148	And F: An
167	will not F: what will
190	house F: place
ii. 11	rased F: razed
12	kept F: held
17	toward F: towards

25	without F: wanting
26	simple F: fond
83	states were F: state was
98	thou met'st me F: I met thee
106	I thank your honour F: God save your lordship
117	cannot stay there F: shall not stay
iii. 6	hereafter! hereafter
24	embrace. F: embrace:
25	Farewell until we meet again F: And take our leave until we meet
iv. 1	Now noble peers F: My lords, at once
4	the F: that
18	honourable F: noble
52	love or hate F: hate or love
73	deed F: thing
82	our helms F: his helm
83	disdain F: disdain'd
85	started F: startled
96	men F: man
v. 31	suspects F: suspect
49-50	Two lines added to Buckingham F: to Mayor's speech
54	meanings have F: meaning hath
57	treasons F: treason
65	case F: cause
68	Which F: But
105	go F: in
vi. 7	desire F: desires
vii. 7	desire F: desires
21	bid F: bade
25	statues F: statuas
29	us'd F: wont
62	suits F: suit
71	love-bed F: day-bed
79	sure F: sore
96	ornaments F: ornament
124	The F: This
	his F: her
125	His F: Her
126	His F: Her
182	off F: by
203	this care F: those cares
213	know whe'r F: whether
219	him F: them
222	stones F: stone
223	entreaties F: entreats

IV. i. 8   farther F: further
        39   thy F: the
        60   brains F: brain
        89   *Dor.* F: *Q. Eliz.*
        97   Stay, yet F: Stay yet,
    ii. 13   lord F: liege
        44   me, untir'd F: me untir'd
        83   request F: demand
       116   May it please you to resolve me in my suit?
                F: Why, then resolve me whe'r you will,
                or no
   iii. 5   ruthful F: ruthless
        7   Melted F: Melting
       13   And F: Which
       15   one F: once
       30   where, to say the truth, F: how or in what
                place
       31   soon, and F: soon at
       39   this F: the
       40   Britaine F: Breton
       41   husband F: Henry
       43   S. d. Ratcliff F: Catesby
    iv. 34   we F: I
    52-53   53 (52) 52 (53)
       64   The F: Thy
       66   Match'd F: Match
       68   frantic F: tragic
       78   and F: to
       88   wast, a garish flag F: were at breath, a
                bubble
    89-90   90 (89) 89 (90) F
       89   dignity, a breath, a bubble, F: dignity, a
                garish flag
       93   be thy two sons F: are thy children
       94   says F: cries
  102-104   she F: one
      107   wast F: wert
      120   sweeter F: fairer
      127   clients F: client
      130   will F: do
      141   Where 't F: Where
      175   with F: in
      187   more behold F: look upon
      200   more F: moe
      212   a royal princess F: of royal blood
      216   birth F: births
      225   hand F: hands

	lanch'd F: lanc'd
262	so F: too
294	gives F: give
324	love F: loan
349	vail F: wail
364-366	(lines transposed)
370	lordly F: holy
376	it F: that
379	didst fear . . . with F: hadst fear'd . . . by
381	Thou hadst not F: Had not been
386	two F: too
387	the F: a
393	with F: in
404	dear F: pure
418	found F: fond
420	you F: thee
502	elder brother F: brother there
518	lord F: liege
528	his course again for Bretagne F: away for Brittany
v. 2	deadly F: bloody
V. i. 3	the most deadly F: this most bloody
10	fellow F: fellows
11	is F: is, my lord,
15	and F: or
24	in F: on
ii. 11	centry F: centre
iii. 20	tract F: track
40	Sweet Blunt, make some good means to speak with him F: Good Captain Blunt, bear my good night to him
46	dew F: air
83	noble F: loving
105	noise F: thoughts
130	king F: the king
132	in F: on
140	in F: on
143	lance F: pointless lance
153	laid F: lead
177	fall F: falls
186	Great reason. Why? F: Great reason why:
187	What? F: What!
200	Throng all F: Throng
202	shall F: will
221	'Tis F: It is
228	and F: the
240	upon F: on

256   swear F: sweat
263   quits F: quit
298   the F: this
305   so F: too
328   seas F: sea
352   helps F: helms
iv. 28   become F: becomes

APPENDIX D

Suggestions for Collateral Reading

W. Hazlitt: *Characters of Shakespear's Plays* [1817]. Everyman edition, p. 73 ff.

Lowell, J. R.: *Shakespeare's Richard III* (1883). In *Last Literary Essays*. [Expresses doubt concerning Shakespeare's authorship.]

R. G. Moulton: *Shakespeare as a Dramatic Artist.* 1885.

Edward Dowden: *Shakespeare; His Mind and Art.* 12th ed., London, 1901. Chap. IV.

F. E. Schelling: *The English Chronicle Play,* 1902.

Stopford A. Brooke: *On Ten Plays of Shakespeare.* New York, 1905. Chap. IV.

Sir Clements R. Markham: *Richard III; His Life and Character.* London, 1906. [A favorable view of Richard in the light of modern historical research.]

G. B. Churchill: *Richard III up to Shakespeare,* 1907.

G. P. Baker: *The Development of Shakespeare as a Dramatist.* 1907.

H. H. Furness, Jr.: *A New Variorum Edition of Shakespeare. Richard III.* Philadelphia, 1909.

L. L. Schücking: *Character Problems in Shakespeare's Plays.* New York, 1922.

E. K. Chambers: *Shakespeare; a Survey.* London, 1925, pp. 10-20.

INDEX OF WORDS GLOSSED

(Figures in full-faced type refer to page numbers)

bottled: **26** (I. iii. 242)

bought and sold: **136** (V. iii. 306)

bowels: **123** (V. ii. 3)

brave: **100** (IV. iii. 57)

brav'd: **135** (V. iii. 280)

brawl: **29** (I. iii. 324)

breathing: **2** (I. i. 21)

breathing-while: **19** (I. iii. 60)

Brecknock: **97** (IV. ii. 121)

Britaine (adj.): **99** (IV. iii. 40)

Britaine (noun): **137** (V. iii. 325)

broken rancour: **50** (II. ii. 117)

Buckingham: **70** (III. iii. 17)

bulk: **31** (I. iv. 40)

Burgundy: **30** (I. iv. 10)

but: **10** (I. ii. 77); **27** (I. iii. 287)

by: **53** (II. iii. 43)

by mighty suit: **81** (III. vii. 45)

by'r: **52** (II. iii. 4)

cacodemon: **22** (I. iii. 144)

caitiff: **104** (IV. iv. 101)

capable: **63** (III. i. 155)

caparison: **136** (V. iii. 290)

care-craz'd: **86** (III. vii. 183)

careful: **20** (I. iii. 83)

carnal: **102** (IV. iv. 56)

carping: **77** (III. v. 67)

cast: **139** (V. iv. 9)

castaways: **46** (II. ii. 6)

censures: **51** (II. ii. 144)

centry: **123** (V. ii. 11)

certifies: **65** (III. ii. 10)

chamber: **57** (III. i. 1)

characters: **60** (III. i. 81)

charge: **84** (III. vii. 130)

check'd: **85** (III. vii. 149)

Chertsey: **8** (I. ii. 29)

circumstance: **10** (I. ii. 77)

cited up: **30** (I. iv. 14)

close: **94** (IV. ii. 35)

closure: **70** (III. iii. 10)

cloudy: **50** (II. ii. 112)

clout: **23** (I. iii. 174)

cockatrice: **91** (IV. i. 54)

cock-shut time: **127** (V. iii. 70)

cog: **19** (I. iii. 48)

compass: **27** (I. iii. 284)

competitors: **119** (IV. iv. 505)

complots: **64** (III. i. 192)

compounded: **43** (II. i. 75)

conceit: **72** (III. iv. 49)

condition: **85** (III. vii. 142); **106** (IV. iv. 158)

conduct: **3** (I. i. 45)

confines: **100** (IV. iv. 3)

consequence: **93** (IV. ii. 15)

consistory: **51** (II. ii. 150)

consorted: **73** (III. iv. 70)

contract: **86** (III. vii. 178)

contract by deputy: **80** (III. vii. 6)

conversation: **76** (III. v. 30)

conveyance: **110** (IV. iv. 284)

convict: **36** (I. iv. 190)

cope withal: **137** (V. iii. 316)

costard: **35** (I. iv. 160)

counted: **91** (IV. i. 46)

Countess Richmond: **18** (I. iii. 20)

cousins: **46** (II. ii. 8)

covert'st: **76** (III. v. 32)

coward conscience: **132** (V. iii. 180)

cozen'd: **108** (IV. iv. 223)

craz'd: **101** (IV. iv. 17)

crew: **121** (IV. v. 15)

cried on: **134** (V. iii. 232)

crimes: **10** (I. ii. 76)

Crosby house: **15** (I. ii. 213)

cross: **61** (III. i. 126)

crosses: **57** (III. i. 4)

cross-row: **3** (I. i. 55)

crown: **66** (III. ii. 43)

cry mercy: **133** (V. iii. 225)

cue: **72** (III. iv. 26)

sharing: **23** (I. iii. 159)
should soonest: **71** (III. iv. 9)
shrift: **74** (III. iv. 95)
shriving: **69** (III. ii. 114)
sign: **78** (III. v. 78)
signiory: **101** (IV. iv. 36)
sit: **63** (III. i. 173)
six Richmonds: **139** (V. iv. 11)
slave of nature: **25** (I. iii. 230)
slower: **11** (I. ii. 117)
slug: **58** (III. i. 22)
smoothing: **13** (I. ii. 169)
snow in harvest: **38** (I. iv. 252)
so: **108** (IV. iv. 210)
soft: **29** (I. iii. 339)
solace: **53** (II. iii. 30)
some: **59** (III. i. 64)
soothe: **28** (I. iii. 298)
sop: **35** (I. iv. 163)
sort: **51** (II. ii. 147); **53** (II. iii. 36); **137** (V. iii. 317)
spent: **68** (III. ii. 88)
spleen: **138** (V. iii. 351)
splinter'd: **50** (II. ii. 118)
spoil: **111** (IV. iv. 291)
spoil'd: **123** (V. ii. 8)
sportive: **1** (I. i. 14)
spurn at: **37** (I. iv. 207)
stall'd: **24** (I. iii. 206)
stands . . . upon: **95** (IV. ii. 58)
statues: **80** (III. vii. 25)
staves: **127** (V. iii. 65)
stay: **48** (II. ii. 74)
stay'd: **106** (IV. iv. 153)
still: **66** (III. ii. 52)
Stony-Stratford: **54** (II. iv. 1)
stopt in: **31** (I. iv. 38)
straight: **82** (III. vii. 69)
straitly: **4** (I. i. 85)
stroke of four: **65** (III. ii. 5)
suborn: **98** (IV. iii. 4)

success: **109** (IV. iv. 237)
successively: **84** (III. vii. 134)
sudden: **29** (I. iii. 346)
suddenly: **117** (IV. iv. 452)
suggestion: **68** (III. ii. 100)
sullen: **92** (IV. i. 101)
sure: **67** (III. ii. 83)
surfeit: **24** (I. iii. 197)
suspects: **20** (I. iii. 89)
swear: **134** (V. iii. 256)
swelling: **42** (II. i. 51)

tall: **35** (I. iv. 157)
tear-falling: **95** (IV. ii. 65)
teen: **92** (IV. i. 96)
tell: **135** (V. iii. 277)
tells: **34** (I. iv. 122)
tempers: **3** (I. i. 65)
tempest: **120** (IV. iv. 522)
tender: **115** (IV. iv. 406)
tendering: **3** (I. i. 44)
testy: **72** (III. iv. 37)
tetchy: **106** (IV. iv. 169)
that: **13** (I. ii. 163)
the time: **128** (V. iii. 93)
there is no more but so: **96** (IV. ii. 79)
this: **3** (I. i. 62)
thraldom: **39** (I. iv. 258)
thrall: **91** (IV. i. 45)
timeless: **11** (I. ii. 118)
to: **48** (II. ii. 67); **65** (III. ii. 27)
to the death: **66** (III. ii. 55)
touch: **10** (I. ii. 71)
toy: **61** (III. i. 114)
toys: **3** (I. i. 60)
tract: **125** (V. iii. 20)
troubled: **128** (V. iii. 105)
troublous: **52** (II. iii. 9)
Turks: **76** (III. v. 40)
type: **109** (IV. iv. 245)

unblown: **100** (IV. iv. 10)
unfashionable: **2** (I. i. 22)
unfelt imaginations: **33** (I. iv. 80)